# China's Apprentice

## Bruce Simpson

ABC BOOKS

This book is dedicated to the memory of those diggers who returned after the hell of Gallipoli and France to carry their swags during the Great Depression.

Published by ABC Books for the
AUSTRALIAN BROADCASTING CORPORATION
GPO Box 9994 Sydney NSW 2001

Copyright © Bruce Simpson 2001
Copyright © illustrations Bruno Grasswill 2001

*First published August 2001*

All rights reserved. No part of this publication may be reproduced, stored in a retrieval system or transmitted in any form or by any means, electronic, mechanical, photocopying, recording or otherwise, without the prior written permission of the Australian Broadcasting Corporation.

National Library of Australia
Cataloguing-in-Publication entry
Simpson, Bruce (Bruce F.), 1923– .
   Chilla's apprentice.
   ISBN 0 7333 1014 1.
   I. Australian Broadcasting Corporation. II. Title.
A823.3

*Set in 11/13 pt Baskerville by*
*Midland Typesetters, Maryborough, Victoria*
*Colour separations by Colorwize, Adelaide*
*Printed and bound in Australia by*
*Griffin Press, Adelaide*

5 4 3 2 1

# Acknowledgments

I would gratefully like to acknowledge the help given to me by the following people: Gordon Gaffney, OAM, of Tamworth, NSW; Colin Newsome of Glen Innes, NSW; Broughton Carter of Moree, NSW; Bill Gammage of the Australian National University, Canberra, ACT; Dannielle Heffernan of the shire office, Moree, NSW; Bruce Amos of Moree, NSW; Don Wall of Mona Vale, NSW; George Cooney of Bribie Island, Qld; and the staff of the Caboolture Council Library, Caboolture, Qld.

Books by the same author

*The Territory Rouseabout and Other Humorous Verses*
*Packhorse Drover*
*In Leichhardt's Footsteps*
*Hell, Highwater and Hard Cases*
Co-editor of *A Thousand Campfires*

# Author's Note

This book is not a serious attempt to analyse the causes and/or effects of the Great Depression of the 1930s. It is the story of a couple of hard cases and their battle to survive during one of the most traumatic periods in Australian history. With the exception of political figures, the characters in this book bear no relation to any person living or dead.

The stanza on page 11 and the poem on pages 165–7 were written by the author. The two lines of song on page 126 were part of a song the author heard as a lad. The chorus of the song on pages 132–3 was picked up by the author many years ago in Camooweal; the rest of the words are his.

# 1

Snowy and I were down on our luck; in fact, we were up the proverbial creek without a paddle. We sat on the low pub verandah and contemplated the future – at least, I did; Snowy didn't seem bothered about it. But then Snowy never appeared to worry about anything. He was one of those characters who couldn't care whether the cow calved or broke its neck, as the saying goes.

We had left our swags down at the waterhole where we were camped. Every day we wandered up town in the hope that something would turn up. I stretched out my legs and gloomily inspected the dilapidated state of my boots. Snowy was gazing across the dusty main street of the little town. He looked at me and said cheerfully, 'She'll be right, mate, something will turn up, you'll see.'

'The way we're going it's likely to be our bloody toes.'

'Don't worry. As my old mate Chilla used to say, things are never that bad that they mightn't get worse.'

'That's a bloody lot of good when you've virtually got the backside out of your trousers.'

Snowy often quoted this Chilla, much as the Chinese quoted Chairman Mao. According to Snowy, the pair had knocked around together when the Great Depression was at its worst. By all accounts, Chilla was a man of great ability and even greater sagacity. He was also a bush philosopher, it was apparent.

'You know,' Snowy said, 'I did a long apprenticeship in the survival trade under old Chilla. I never went short of a feed when I was with him. The wily old bastard used to keep a few dead flies in a matchbox. He'd go into a cafe and order a feed, then he would put his tobacco and match tin on the table so they'd be handy to light up when he had finished his meal. He would wait until he'd almost

*It worked every time. God knows how many free meals we got with Chilla's flies. We had to be careful, though, not to hit the same place twice.*

cleaned up his plate, then when no one was looking he'd drop a couple of flies onto the remaining tucker and stir them around a bit. As soon as the waitress came out of the kitchen, Chilla would demand to see the boss.

'It worked every time. God knows how many free meals we got with Chilla's flies. We had to be careful, though, not to hit the same place twice.'

'It would be handy to have him here. What happened to him?'

Snowy shook his head. 'I dunno, I lost track of him. I think he may be dead. If he's not, he'll be up to his old tricks somewhere.'

Snowy took out his tobacco tin and carefully rolled a smoke. It ended up a little thicker than a toothpick. He lit it and, clearing his throat, asked, 'Did I ever tell you about the time Chilla and I were short of the ready in a small town near the coast?'

I shook my head. 'I don't think so.'

'Well,' Snow began, 'we were really on the bone of our backsides. Compared to our situation then, Shit Creek was Shangri-La. Chilla had pulled the fly trick on the one cafe in town. There were two pubs, but he'd never use the flies at pubs – he reckoned pubs were places of business. We had worked the lost dog racket a couple of times, but . . .'

'Hang on, Snow, what's this lost dog business?'

'Well, for some reason, when most people lose a dog they put up a notice in the butcher's window – as though they expected the bloody dog to go to the shop for meat, read the bloody sign and go home. Chilla would always bludge bones from the butcher so he could keep an eye out. The bones made damn good soup, anyway, and the butcher knew we always got dog bones from him. After a few days of that, Chilla would sneak up town at night and knock off a spoilt-looking mutt from a flash house. All we had to do then was wait for the reward notice. We picked up a few quid like that, then the game got a bit too hot. Chilla ran into a bloody great Alsatian one night that almost tore his trousers off. After that, he decided to give dognapping away.'

Listening to Snow's yarns was a great tonic, and he needed little encouragement to continue ...

> A day or two later we were walking up the main street of this place when Chilla stopped. I could see he was looking at a shop opposite one of the pubs. A ladder was leaning against one wall and it was obvious the shop was being painted. I couldn't see anything unusual about it. Chilla shook his head. 'You look but you do not see,' he says to me sadly. 'That ladder was in the same place yesterday; there's something wrong there.' Chilla scratched his chin for a minute or two, then asked me if I had enough money left to buy two beers. I told him I had but did not intend to squander it on beer. 'We are not squandering it,' Chilla said, 'we're making a business investment.'
>
> As we walked into the public bar, I noticed that Chilla was limping a bit. The publican behind the bar greeted us warily – times were like that then – but he thawed out a bit as we yarned. Chilla went to the 'Gents' and when he returned the man behind the bar asked him what he'd done to his leg. Chilla took a sip of beer. 'France,' he said quietly. The publican started to ask something, but Chilla put his hand up and said, 'I never talk about it. It's hard enough to get a job without advertising things like that.' We talked about the crop prices, then Chilla said, 'Who's doing the painting over the road?'
>
> The publican explained gleefully that no one was at the moment – the painter had fallen off a ladder and broken an ankle. Apparently the owner and the publican did not hit it off. He added that a new tenant was due to open a business in the shop the following week and the signwriter was due in a few days time.
>
> Chilla was pretty casual about it all, but before we left he asked the publican where he could find the shop owner. He was told that the miserable bastard drank at the other hotel, and could usually be found there with his snout in

the trough after five every afternoon. We said farewell to the publican and headed back to camp, picking up some bones from the butcher on the way. When we got back, Chilla asked me if I'd ever done any painting. I told him I'd slapped a bit of paint on fences and on a few sheds. He nodded and seemed pleased by that, but didn't say anything. Five o'clock came and went with no move from Chilla.

When I asked him what the hell was going on, he told me impatience was one of the deadly sins. I didn't know if it was or not, but I'd learnt never to doubt old Chilla's word. I said, 'Aren't we going to apply for the job of painting the shop?'

'No,' he said, 'they are going to ask us to paint the shop.'

Well, he could see I hadn't cottoned on, so he said to me, 'Suppose you saw two men walking down the street and one was a policeman. How would you know which one was the copper?'

I laughed. 'That's easy. He's the bloke in the uniform.'

'Good,' said Chilla. 'Now, what if you saw a bloke in greasy overalls?'

I told him I reckoned he'd be a mechanic.

'Very good,' said Chilla. 'Now, get some sleep, we've got work to do later.'

Chilla woke me up in the middle of the night and told me to get a set of old clothes out of my swag. I saw that he had done the same and had the billy boiling for a drink of tea. Finding old clothes was no trouble – that was all I had. We had a drink of tea, then Chilla told me to grab a spur and follow him. I had a fair idea what he was up to, but the spur had me buggered. Twenty minutes later we were at the back of the half-painted shop. Chilla struck a match, and selecting a few tins of different coloured paint, he told me to open them with the spur. Chilla laid the clothing we had brought down flat, then with a paint stirrer he flicked and dripped paint on both outfits. We tidied up and made a beeline for our camp. We had to walk with our arms outstretched, holding the clobber away from the gear we were wearing – Chilla reckoned buggering up one set of clothes was all the job was worth. Come to think of it, I reckon we would have frightened a year's growth out of anyone we bumped into that night.

When we got back to camp Chilla spread the clothes out on bushes to dry. We put the billy on again and Chilla sat there drinking the tea and chuckling to himself.

'Never think, young Snowy,' he said, 'that your head is just a place to park your hat. Remember, always keep your eyes and ears open and think before you say anything.'

'Did you get the job?' I asked my mate.

Yeah, but we had to wait until five to see the owner. In the morning Chilla went out shooting. We had an old single-shot .22 with us. About nine o'clock he comes back with a plain turkey. 'Hang on,' I said to him, 'it's illegal to shoot them.'

'I know,' he said, 'but you can shoot them in self defence. This bloody bird nearly got me. Put that big billy on and get plenty of hot water. You can pluck and clean the bludger and we'll have a late lunch of roast turkey.'

A bit after five we got done up in our painting gear and went up to the pub where the shop owner drank. Luckily we hadn't been in the place before, due to being stony. Before we got there Chilla gave me the drum.

'If you see anyone looking at us, don't crack a lay – leave the spruiking to me.'

We walked into the bar and ordered small beers. 'Drink slowly,' Chilla hissed at me out of the corner of his mouth. I could see this bloke eyeing us off, and after a minute, around he came.

'You fellows are painters?' he asked.

'Well,' said Chilla, 'we're not going to a fancy dress ball.'

The bloke laughed. 'Sorry, I didn't mean to offend. It's just that I've got a job for you if you're interested.'

'Aw, I dunno,' Chilla said to him. 'We're just here for a few days spell. We've got a big job half finished up north and all our gear is back there.'

'That's no problem,' the bloke tells us, and gives us all the information we already know. 'How much would you want to do the job?' he asked.

Chilla fiddled with his empty glass for a bit, then said, 'Oh, three quid a day – each,' he quickly added as the bloke nodded his head.

The shop owner gulped, but Chilla knew he had him by the short and curlies. They shook hands and Chilla said, 'Right, let's have a drink on it. Your shout, boss.'

We got two and half days out of it, then shot through and headed up north.

'Well,' I said, 'you'd better put some of Chilla's survival techniques to work now.'

Snowy thought for a while. 'It's bloody hot, eh?'

I looked at him in disgust. I already knew it was hot – it was also very humid; we weren't all that far from the Queensland coast. Snowy got to his feet.

'I've got an idea. I've got enough on me for a couple of beers. Come on.'

I stood up and followed Chilla's apprentice into the bar. The place was almost empty. The publican stopped polishing an already spotless bar.

'What's it to be, gents?'

'A couple of beers please, boss,' Snowy ordered. 'A man could perish in weather like this.'

'True,' said the publican. 'Do you think it will rain?'

Snowy rubbed his left shoulder. 'Yeah, I reckon it's going to teem. This old bunged-up wing of mine never lets me down.'

'You're probably right. They say there's a cyclone likely to cross the coast within the next few days.'

'There you are, then,' said Snow. 'We'll probably get plenty of rain and some high wind here, but nothing to worry about. You would have had the roof checked, I suppose?'

The publican looked at Snow. 'Roof checked? What do you mean?'

'Oh, nothing. Sorry, it's none of my business.'

'Come on, I want to know what you meant. What could be wrong with the roof?'

'Well,' said Snow reluctantly, 'it's just that the timber in these old roofs dries out and shrinks, leaving the iron a bit loose. In a high wind it only takes one sheet to lift and your roof is gone. All you have to do to fix things is to get someone to tighten the roofing nails.'

'Jesus Christ,' said the publican. 'Nobody told me that when I bought the place, and there's no bloody carpenter in town.'

'That's typical of real estate people,' said Snow. 'But you don't really need a carpenter ... anyone who can use a hammer should be able to do the job,' he added casually.

The publican nodded, then looked at us. 'If you blokes aren't doing anything at the moment could you help me out?'

Snow looked at me. 'What do you think?'

With some difficulty I kept a straight face and nodded agreement.

'The job has to be finished as soon as possible,' Snow said, as though talking to himself. 'I think we'll do it on contract. If you've got a couple of hammers and a ladder, all we'll need is a pound of roofing nails from the store.'

The publican agreed that a contract was the best way to go and inquired about price. Snowy rubbed his chin for a bit, then said, 'Well, we're camped down the creek at the moment. If you let us camp on the back verandah it'll help us to work faster, and if you toss in tucker and a few beers after we knock off, I reckon we can do the whole roof for ten quid.'

It seemed to be a good deal for the publican and he shook hands on it with both of us and shouted us a beer.

'Right,' said Snow, 'we'll get this into us then bring our swags up, and get the roofing nails. We should be ready to start after we have lunch.'

On the way down to our camp I congratulated Snowy on the job he'd done. He grinned at me. 'Chilla once told me that sometimes you have to create a market so you can supply what is needed.'

'Fair enough, but I think you made a mistake on the contract deal.'

He stopped and looked at me. 'So did the publican, but I'm gambling on that cyclone going to buggery so we can take our time on the job while we get fat on pub cooking.'

I had to admit to myself that Snowy had been an outstanding student in the art of survival.

We trudged back and threw our swags on two vacant stretchers on the back verandah. By the time we got the nails and found the hammers and the ladder the lunch bell rang.

'Come on,' said Snow. 'I work better on a full stomach.' We strolled into the pub dining room and sat down. A waitress came in and walked over to our table. She was a tall girl with light auburn hair and a dusting of freckles across her nose. I noticed that she had one green eye while the other one was blue. She looked at us doubtfully.

'Are you guests, or are you paying for the meal?'

Snow looked her over with interest. 'Neither, we're carpenters. We're on staff, just like you.'

The girl looked even more uncertain. 'I'll have to check with the boss. Would you like soup?'

'No thanks,' said Snowy. 'I'll have a Camooweal sandwich.'

'A Camooweal sandwich. What's that?' asked the waitress in a guarded manner.

'Oh, it's a lizard between two sheets of bark,' replied Snow with a cheeky grin. The waitress eyed my companion icily.

'What you'll get is on the menu, and whether you get it on the table or over your head is entirely up to you. If you're not having soup, the lunch menu is silverside and salad.'

Snow, duly chastened, agreed that the silverside would do nicely. I ordered the same and the waitress departed for the kitchen. I told Snowy to pull his head in, or our stay at the pub could be short lived. The waitress returned with two plates of corned beef and rather limp-looking salad.

'The cook said to give you this, and to tell you that if you're not careful you'll be eating it on the woodheap.'

'Don't take any notice of this mate of mine,' I told her. 'He's an out-of-work comedian.' The waitress left us with a toss of her head.

'She'll be right,' said my mate. 'I'll have her eating out of my hand in a few days time.'

'If you're not careful, the only thing you're likely to have in your hand is your head.'

After lunch we got to work.

'We'll do the front verandah first,' Snowy decided. 'It's on the weather side.'

We hauled the ladder around and placed it in position.

'You get the rest of the gear,' Snowy ordered, 'while I climb up and have a gander.'

I returned with the hammers and nails as Snowy scuttled back down the ladder.

'Christ, it'd burn the balls off you up there.'

I climbed up, and as soon as my head rose above the roof level the heat hit me like a blast from a furnace. I climbed down and grinned at my mate. 'Well, boss, what now?'

Snowy thought for a minute or two. 'I'll tell you what we can do until it cools off a bit, we'll see the publican about borrowing a couple of those carpet runners out of the hall, that should help a bit.'

We found the publican and told him of our problem.

'That's no trouble,' he told us, 'but leave it for an hour before you start. The missus likes a bit of a nap after lunch.'

We agreed with alacrity and headed for the bar. At a quarter to three we rolled out the runners and got to work. The roof really did need attention. Almost every nail was loose, and quite a few needed to be replaced. The slight feeling of guilt I had harboured quickly disappeared.

It was bloody hot even with the runners for protection, but I noticed with some relief that a band of cloud was slowly rising along the northern horizon. Perhaps the job would be a little more pleasant on the morrow.

By knock off time we had almost finished the front verandah. We agreed to do the rest of it before breakfast next morning. Snowy, always keen to know where his next meal was coming from, decided we would then get stuck into the roof on the semi-detached kitchen, thus protecting the food source in case the cyclone did its worst.

After a quick shower we just had time for a couple of beers before the gong rang for dinner. We walked into the dining room, which was now well patronised, and sat in the same seats. The waitress took our orders without any of the lunchtime repartee. We were both tired and leg weary from the unaccustomed crouching on the roof. For once Snowy was quite subdued.

The waitress returned to the dining room carrying six full dinner plates. She held two in each hand and another two balanced on her wrists and on the edges of the other plates. Both Snowy and I watched in amazement as she delivered the meals; the only assistance needed was for diners to take the two plates off her wrists.

Later the waitress returned to the room with six full cups of tea. When she came to give us our meals, Snowy complimented her on the performance. I could see she was pleased but she said without any fuss that it was merely practice.

We ate our meal in a leisurely manner and were the last in the room when we finished. Snowy's behaviour had been exemplary, smiling at the waitress and quietly saying please and thank you. I watched with interest, as this was obviously a change of technique. The waitress, however, showed little signs of thawing.

As we were about to leave, Snowy asked the girl her name and was told it was Maisie. Heartened by this information, he inquired when she would be knocking off. Maisie gave him a sharp look and told him the publican did not encourage the staff to fraternise with the guests. Snow, looking a bit like a stunned mullet, sat back and said, 'Oh!'

When we got outside Snowy looked at me. 'What the hell is frat ... whatever she said? I don't want to get into her pants – well, not yet anyway.'

I laughed at his confusion. 'Fraternisation,' I told him, 'is just socialising.'

'Right,' said Snowy. 'I wish people would say what they mean. I'll keep working on her – we've got a few days yet.'

Neither of us felt like a drink, so we retired to our swags and lay smoking. We had both got a fresh tin of fine cut from the publican.

'You know,' my mate mused aloud, 'they reckon smoking is bad for you, but Chilla always said it was those tailormade bastards that did the damage. He always reckoned a smoke was as good as a feed if you were really hungry. Said it took the edge right off your appetite. Old Chilla used to recite a poem about smoking. I'll see if I can remember it, if you'd like to hear it.'

'Right, let her rip, I don't mind listening to poetry.'

Snowy thought for a minute, then started.

> We can all of us smile when we're winning
> And laugh when the world's at our feet,
> We are most of us big-hearted fellas
> When good luck's on our side of the street.
> But give me the man who when losing
> Can still crack a grin and a joke,
> Who can count up his blessings remaining
> And roll up his cares with a smoke.

'Well, what do you think of that?' he asked.

'Quite good. Did he write it?'

'I dunno, he told me he started to smoke on the Peninsula because of the stink of the dead blokes just in front of the trench.'

'You mean Gallipoli?'

'Yeah, but Chilla just said the Peninsula.'

'I thought from what you said he was wounded in France.'

'That's what he said, and if he said that, it would be right. Not that he talked about it at all. I did run into a bloke, though, who was with him over there. He said Chilla went right through the war and was only twenty-two when it finished. He did have a hell of a scar just above his knee. I saw it plenty of times when he was having a dip in the creek. It didn't bother him much. I reckon pound for pound he was the strongest man that I've ever run into.'

'You thought a lot of him, didn't you?'

'Yeah, well, he sorta took me under his wing, you know. I think I told you once I was raised in a Sydney orphanage. It was a tough place, the tucker was rough and light on, and they raised us kids with prayer and a bloody big stick. Honesty is the best policy, they would say, giving you a welt on the arse at the same time, just in case you were thinking of knocking something off. I was fostered out a couple of times but always ended up back at the bloody orphanage. In the end I cleared out and changed my name. I was only about twelve years old, but I was a tough kid, and with hard work and decent tucker I grew a lot and muscled up. I became as fit as a scrub bull, and reckoned I could hold my own.

'Later I told Chilla about honesty being the best policy. He looked at me hard and then he said, "Well, Snow, that's good advice most of the time. But if you're starving, the best policy is to go and get something to eat – any way you can. As long as you don't take it from anyone as badly off as yourself I don't reckon it's a crime. No one should starve in this country. But there are people starving, and that's the greatest crime of all."'

# 2

We smoked in silence for a while. Snowy had told me a lot about himself and Chilla but seldom anything about his childhood. His remarks about the orphanage intrigued me and I decided to quiz him about it. I reckoned we knew each other well enough for it not to cause embarrassment. If he didn't want to talk about it, he would just say so and that would be that. I finished my smoke, dropped the butt in the empty tobacco tin that served as an ashtray and looked over at my mate.

'It must have been hard in that orphanage, Snow. How the hell did you end up there?'

Snowy didn't answer for a minute or two. He put both hands behind his head and stared at the unlined roof above him. 'You know,' he said at last, 'I haven't a bloody clue how I got there. My first clear memories are of the blasted place, but I've got a faint recollection of being with an old lady before that. She may have been my grandmother or an aunt, I don't know. What I'm sure of is that I never met my parents.'

'Christ, Snowy! Didn't anyone ever come to see you?'

'Well, an old bloke did visit the place once and talked to me. I think he was old, anyway, but when you're about five, everyone who isn't in short pants is old.'

'Was he a relative?'

'I'm buggered if I know – he could have been. He must have told me a lot, but I only remember two things. I was born in 1914 and my father was killed in the war. He never mentioned my mother, so I don't know what the story was there. Before he left, he gave me some papers and three medals. The people at the orphanage took them and they've probably still got them. Thinking about it now, I reckon the bloke who came to see me must have been a mate of my father's.'

'Did he ever come to see you again?'

'No. Well, not as far as I know. I was fostered out, of course, and he may have come then. I doubt if the people at the orphanage would have told him where I was.'

'Did they send you to a family?'

'It's a long story. Do you want to hear it?'

I nodded.

Well, I was sent to an Irish couple on a small farm. They didn't have any kids of their own and I think they just wanted some cheap labour. As you know, no farm in Australia could survive without child labour, especially those days. Anyway, this bloke picked me up from a railway station in a spring cart and took me to this farm. They had put me on the train in Sydney and told the guard where to put me off. I was six years old at the time, about that, anyway. It wasn't too bad at first – at least the meals were all right and I had a bed to sleep in.

It was soon pointed out that I had to earn my keep and I discovered that meant working from dawn to dark. Of course, I knew nothing about farming, but I soon worked out that this Irish bloke – Dinny, his wife called him – knew about as much as I did. It was only a small farm, but he tried his hand at everything, and ended up doing nothing right. When talking to me about him, his wife always referred to him as Mr Murphy. I think Murphy's Law was based on his method of farming. He was a great one for poultry – there were ducks, fowls, turkeys, geese and even a bloody peacock on the place. The trouble was he never had enough feed for the poor bastards.

We planted corn in one small paddock, but the cows kept knocking the old fence down and ate most of the crop. He seemed to stuff up everything he touched, and used to rave on about the Government, about the English oppressors and absentee landlords. His wife was a good woman. She must have seen what a hopeless idiot he was, but like him she tended to blame all and sundry for their troubles.

We used to milk about a dozen cows every morning. I'd

bring the cows up to the yards the evening before and pen the calves overnight. As dawn was breaking every morning, I had to go down the paddock and bring the milkers into the cow yard. I never had any boots them days and the frost used to be thick on the grass. To warm my feet up, I'd stick them into fresh pats of warm cow dung.

It did the job but I used to get cow itch on my feet. It would give you hell in hot weather. There was only one bail in the cow yard. Dinny used that, and I had to push a cow up against the yard and milk it there. I used an old stump as a stool and more often than not I'd get kicked arse over head off it.

'Save the milk,' Dinny would yell, and I did my best. It didn't seem to matter if there was a percentage of foreign matter in it, either. We used kerosene tins for milking and after we were finished we would take the milk up to a lean-to shed Dinny called the dairy, and leave it there while we had breakfast. Mrs Murphy was a good cook, no doubt about that. She could knock up a meal out of almost nothing. Seeing as she was married to Murphy, I reckon she got plenty of practice.

Anyway, after breakfast it was my job to separate the cream from the milk. Murphy had an old Alfa Laval separator. I hated that bloody thing, and I hated the name, Alfa bloody Laval. I had to turn the bloody handle of the thing until my bloody arm nearly fell off. Now and again I'd stick a finger under the cream spout and take a good lick to strengthen meself. I don't suppose it was the right thing to do as Murphy had to sell the cream, but then most of Murphy's methods were a long way short of being clean.

After I had finished separating I had to feed the skim milk to the calves and the pigs. Murphy had pigs, of course. I've never known an Irish farmer who didn't have pigs.

The trouble was there was never enough skim milk to go round. One morning the calves would go short; the next morning the pigs missed out. Murphy would keep the cream can in a Coolgardie safe until he had enough to send to the butter factory. After three or four days he would load the can onto the spring cart and take it out to the road that passed the farm. From there it would be picked up and taken to the factory. Murphy was never happy with the cream cheque he received, and at times the cream would be rejected and he cursed all Englishmen and absentee landlords.

I had a good idea where the trouble lay. A Coolgardie safe is a frame with hessian walls kept wet from a water trough above. It works perfectly well as long as the water trough is kept full. Many times I passed the safe to find the walls bone dry. Murphy preferred to blame absentee landlords rather than his own stupidity.

Mind you, they were good people in a lot of ways. It didn't take me long to work Murphy out. He was softer than the staff at the orphanage and a bloody fool to boot. It took me a long time to relate to his wife, though. I'd had nothing to do with women, and kindness just for kindness's sake confused me. In the end, I got to like them both, and I realised that the world was not totally made up of bastards. I learned to shrug off Murphy's faults. After all, it was no skin off my nose if he stuffed things up. At times, though, I felt a bit sorry for his wife. She tried so hard to make a go of things.

At one stage the poultry side of the business was suffering losses from a raiding fox. The various birds were kept in a large netting fenced area, with a bark shed at one end for shade and shelter. In that fowl yard the various birds fought for survival, and for the scraps that were thrown over the fence. Collecting the few eggs the birds laid was a hazardous business in bare feet – the duck and fowl droppings made the enclosure like a mine field.

It was no surprise that birds were disappearing, as the fence was in a bad state of repair. Whenever the fox paid a visit, the bloody peacock and the geese would kick up a hell of a racket. Murphy would yell out to the dog, 'Sool 'em, Tiger.' And Tiger, a dog of doubtful breeding, would leave his kennel, scratch a few fleas, lick his backside and then, like Murphy, go back to sleep.

This went on for a while, then, at his wife's insistence,

Murphy went into action. He had an old twelve gauge shotgun, and loading this, he went into the fowl yard one night to wait for the fox. I thought it would make more sense to plant outside, but I knew Murphy well enough to keep my mouth shut. All the birds in the fowl yard were camped under the shed, some on the ground and some on perches, and of course the fox came in through the back of the shed. Murphy took rapid aim and fired. When the feathers cleared, I saw that two hens and four ducks had been blown to blazes, while the fox had departed without a scratch.

I was ordered to salvage what I could from the disaster. I selected three of the less mutilated birds, and, taking them over to the woodheap, I chopped their heads off and drained out what little blood remained in them. Mrs Murphy had a tub of hot water ready. I tossed them in and then after plucking and cleaning the scrawny bastards I took them into the kitchen. We dined on poultry that night, spitting out the stray shot as we ate.

Murphy used to sell his pigs and calves in town. He'd put them in a wire-netting cage on the back of the spring cart. It was the worst example of a stock crate I ever saw. He would then head for the nearest town, about ten miles away. Loading the livestock onto the back of the spring cart was bad enough; it was sometimes even more difficult to keep them there. Murphy always went on his own and I don't think he ever got to town with a full load. The calves that escaped would come home looking for their mothers, but the pigs must have had enough of Murphy, for we never saw any of them again.

He obviously got a grog or two into him on those trips. If he had made a good sale he would arrive a bit under the weather, and would bring a couple of bottles of stout home with him. On those nights he would sit at the kitchen table drinking and cursing the English and in particular the Black and Tans. I didn't know who the hell they were, but he had a bloody bee in his bonnet about them. When this happened Mrs Murphy would take me out of the room and send me to bed, saying, 'You mustn't take any notice of Mr Murphy when he's in his cups.'

One night he sang a song called 'Kevin Barry'. His wife became very upset. She called me into the front room and made me swear on a bible that I would never ever tell anyone what I had heard. I couldn't work out what all the fuss was about – it wasn't a bad song.

One day after I'd been there about six months, I saw this copper riding up the road to Murphy's place. He looked very smart in his slouch hat and polished leggings, but I reckoned he was trouble. I wasn't sure whether he was coming to arrest Murphy for singing that song, or to take me back to the orphanage.

I decided not to wait around to find out, so I scarpered and planted behind the dairy. Peering around the side of the shed, I saw him go inside, and after a bit Mrs Murphy came looking for me. It wasn't hard to find me, as hiding places around the farm were like Murphy's brains, few and far between.

'The policeman wants to talk to you,' she told me.

I followed her up to the house with my tail between my legs. It's back to that bloody orphanage, I thought to myself. When I got inside, the copper looked me over. 'How old are you, sonny?'

I gulped. 'Six and a half, I think.'

Mrs Murphy chipped in. 'The policeman says you have to go to school.'

'Where?' I asked.

'There's a new school about three miles away,' the policeman informed us. 'It's been open for most of this year.'

I felt a flood of relief. But I could see that Murphy wasn't too happy about the idea. He would now have to share his unpaid worker with the Education Department. Finally it was agreed that I should go to school, and the copper left to advise the teacher he would have a new student the following Monday. I had done two years of schooling at the orphanage so I reckoned I would pick the work up all right. It was decided that I could ride to school on Murphy's old pony mare, a skinny little brute called Mrs Maloney. I would have to ride her bareback, of course.

On the following Monday morning after I had finished the separating, I mounted my ancient steed and set out with high hopes and a lunch of jam sandwiches. The greeting I got at school didn't come as any surprise to me, having experienced the regime at the orphanage.

A lot of the kids were big rough farm boys of thirteen or fourteen who were still in the lower grades. They made me welcome by playing football with my jam sandwiches and poked fun at the bony Mrs Maloney. I was christened the Irish tyke, and it was plain that as a new boy I was at the bottom of the pecking order – I'd be the butt of every joke anyone liked to play. A group of the older louts started a chant.

> *Irishmen, Irishmen, bow down your heads,*
> *There's cows in your parlour and pigs in your beds.*

Well, the Murphys weren't the greatest family in the world, but they were the only family I had, so I got stuck into the bastards. They belted hell out of me, of course, but I was tough and always came back for more. After a few days they got sick of punching the living daylights out of me and gave it away.

The teacher was only a young bloke from the city. He just couldn't handle the bigger louts, and they made his life a misery, both in school and out. He used to ride a bike out from the town every day. These big kids used to ambush him with shanghais and they'd put tacks on the road to puncture his tyres. After I was at school for a month or so, he had a nervous breakdown and had to leave. The Education Department must have contained a few brainy fellers back then, because the replacement they sent out was a big ex-footballer.

The first day, he locked the doors and lined all the big kids up and gave 'em a flogging. He never had no more trouble after that.

I got on pretty well with my school work, but still had a lot of work to do on the farm when I got home. I mustered the cows on old Mrs Maloney, penned the calves, chopped wood, gathered kindling for the morning and cleaned the glass on each kerosene light. The new teacher always gave us homework, so after tea I got down to it on the kitchen table.

After a while Mrs Murphy used to come and sit with me. I thought she was there to help me if I got stuck with something, but then it suddenly dawned on me that she was trying to learn from what I was doing. Without being obvious, I sorta made it easier for her to see the work. She must have woken up to what I was up to, for one night she blurted out that she couldn't read and write. We agreed then to work together each night. I quite enjoyed it, not because it made me feel superior, but because we had a common bond. From that time on, she and I became good mates.

Murphy was still lurching from one disaster to another with his farming efforts. He planted pumpkins, but the pigs broke out of the sty and rooted all the vines out. Towards the end of the year he was going to make a killing with watermelons for Christmas, but he messed around so long getting the ground ready that the vines on other farms were flowering as he planted the seeds. He did get a fair drop of melons, but by the time they were ready, the horse had bolted, so to speak. It was after New Year and everyone was sick of watermelons. But for once the poultry had more to eat than they could handle, and collecting the eggs became even more hazardous.

I had learnt very early in life to keep my mouth shut and my eyes and ears open. At school I picked up a lot of farming information, and during the Christmas holidays I would drop hints to Murphy about doing things differently. He didn't take a lot of notice at first, but gradually he tried a few of my ideas, and when they worked, he was very quick to claim them as his own.

Mrs Murphy began to confide in me more and more.

Sometimes after the evening meal she would talk about Ireland. I could see she was homesick.

She said she had come out to Australia on an immigrant ship when she was a girl of thirteen. Her parents had died shortly after arriving. I got the idea she had married Murphy to get a roof over her head. She used to tell me of the plans she had when the farm came good and how she would like to see Ireland again.

One night I said, 'I suppose Mr Murphy would like to see the old country again too.'

She gave a funny sort of laugh. 'I suppose he would, seeing as the poor man has never been there.'

'But I thought . . .'

She stopped me. 'You mustn't take any notice of Mr Murphy. There's no harm in the poor man.'

On Christmas Eve Mrs Murphy insisted we all go to the Catholic church for Mass. Murphy harnessed Paddy, his only work horse, in the spring cart and we set out, scrubbed and wearing the best clothes we had. I noticed Mrs Murphy sent Murphy to confession afterwards.

Mrs Murphy gave me a brand new pair of pants. It was the first time I had ever received a Christmas present. She used to give me a treat, a hot mug of cocoa, if I got wet coming home from school. I'd never seen cocoa before and I used to chase showers on old Mrs Maloney to get wet enough for that cocoa. Sometimes if I missed a shower, I would jam the old nag under saplings and shake them until I was wet enough to qualify.

I stayed with the Murphys for about three years, and the farm gradually improved as I had more to do with what was done. They were a middle aged couple and apparently couldn't have kids of their own. Towards the end of my stay there, Mrs Murphy was talking of adopting me into the family.

I thought about it a lot and thought it wasn't a bad idea. It would mean I would get away from the orphanage for good. I also thought that I could help a lot to make a go of the farm.

# 3

Next morning we were up at daybreak and had finished the verandah roof before breakfast. When the gong went, we saddled up to an old fashioned pub breakfast of rolled oats followed by steak and eggs. The eggs were overcooked and Snowy shook his head. A cook who couldn't fry eggs was a dead loss, he said.

'Christ! You've only had your feet under the table for one day and you're complaining already,' I told him.

He took the rebuke with a grin. 'Well, I was being honest, and honesty is the best policy, they used to tell me.'

Maisie seemed more relaxed in our company and laughed when Snowy told her we would be starting work on the kitchen roof as soon as we'd finished our meal.

'What's so funny?' Snow wanted to know. 'I thought the noise might upset you.'

'It won't worry me,' Maisie said. 'But you'd better watch out for the cook.'

'Is that right? A bit of a dragon is she?'

'I'm afraid she's a real tartar. No one here likes her. It would be a blessing if she pulled out.'

'You may leave *that*', said Snowy, 'in my capable hands.'

I looked at my mate. 'Snowy, we're on a good thing here, thanks to you. Why jeopardise it by interfering with the staff?'

Snowy grinned broadly. 'We must plan for the future. Leave everything to me.'

We shifted the ladder and gear over to the kitchen. Snowy threw his hammer onto the roof, then climbed up after it. There was a fair bit of cloud cover overhead, so we dispensed with the carpet runners. This of course added to the noise. I pulled my boots off, but noticed that Snowy was stamping around and banging away like a mob of billy goats on a tin roof.

It didn't take long to flush the cook out. She stood arms akimbo and glared up at us.

'What do you pair of bloody idiots think you're doing?' she stormed.

'It's better to have a bit of noise now', I said, 'than to lose the roof later.'

'We are following orders,' Snow added. 'Why don't you do the same? Go back to your bloody kitchen and read a cookbook – you may learn how to cook eggs.'

'Don't you cheek me, I know what you're up to. You might fool the boss, but don't think you can pull the wool over my eyes.'

'That's a crying shame,' Snow told her. 'It may improve your looks.'

'Right,' screeched the cook, 'I'm off to see the boss.'

I heard laughter from the kitchen beneath. Maisie was obviously enjoying the show.

I glanced over at my mate. 'You'll have to do a bit of talking to get out of this,' I told him. 'My advice is to get your boots off and your head down.'

Snowy did as I suggested and we were working flat out when the publican arrived.

He stood and shouted up to us, 'Hey, I want to talk to you men.'

Snowy must have a guardian angel. At that moment a gust of wind lifted a sheet of iron slightly – it began to rattle, and Snowy shouted to me, 'Quick, Simmo, get over there and nail that down.' He looked down at the publican. 'We're going flat out to finish the kitchen roof. If this cyclone hits, we don't want to be without hot meals, do we?'

It took the wind right out of the publican's sails. 'Well,' he said rather lamely, 'I can't have you upsetting the staff. The cook has just given two days notice.'

'Don't worry,' said Snowy, 'I can take over the kitchen when she leaves. I've cooked for shearers, so I'll be able to handle the job. Simmo here can do the rest of the roof if it isn't finished by then.'

The publican went back inside. I felt a bit sorry for him. He was not a bad bloke, but he was putty in the hands of Chilla's apprentice. After a few minutes the cook stormed back to the kitchen. Snowy, who could never resist temptation, called down, 'Make sure you leave the kitchen clean. I'll be taking over, you know.'

The cook's reply was picturesque but unprintable.

In contrast to the day before, the cloud cover made the conditions quite pleasant. We worked steadily on the kitchen and by lunchtime had it finished. We moved the gear over to the back verandah and were about to start on it when the lunch bell rang.

Maisie greeted us with a wide grin when we sat down at our usual table. She looked at Snowy. 'Can you really cook? I hear you're going to take over in the kitchen.'

'Can I cook!' he replied. 'You might as well ask a wild duck can it swim, or a wild cat can it fight.'

'I suppose that means yes. There's no soup today – just curry and rice.'

We told her that would be fine, as long as it didn't include ground glass. Quite pleased with our morning's work, we enjoyed the lunch.

'Well,' said Snowy, 'the old girl can certainly cook a curry.'

Maisie, who was now definitely on our side, laughed. 'Would you like me to relay that compliment to the cook?'

'You'd better not,' my mate said. 'Anyway, the rice was a bit gluey.'

After we finished lunch we strolled on to the back verandah and settled down for an hour or so on our swags. We both agreed that the publican's wife was a woman of great common sense. In Snowy's opinion only a fool would work in the heat of the day, a conviction no doubt picked up from the worthy Chilla. Snowy seemed in good spirits, so I asked him what had gone wrong with the Murphys' adoption plans.

He seemed hesitant at first, then said ...

Oh, I don't mind talking about it. It's just that I feel it was in some way my fault. You see there was a lot of sickness about those days, and because of poverty or the lack of treatment, there were a lot of home cures. Very few people ever went to hospital. Mrs Murphy had a lot of home remedies, including a dose of castor oil every Saturday morning. Christ! I hated that blue bottle. She treated a cold with camphor, and rubbed my chest with kerosene and olive oil every night. For boils or school sores, she made up soap and sugar poultices. I reckon those poultices would pull a cow out of a bloody bog. Diphtheria was around and people used to paint kids' throats with kerosene on a feather. I think some of the bloody cures then were worse than the diseases. Anyway, I didn't get diphtheria, but I did get measles, and I got 'em real bad.

Mrs Murphy kept me home from school and put me to bed. She said I had a high temperature, although she didn't have a therm ... whatever you call it. Anyway, I was real crook. Murphy was away with the spring cart, helping a bloke put down a dam about twelve miles away. When the time came to get the cows, it was drizzling. Mrs Murphy said she would walk down and bring them in. She came back a little later shaking and white faced, saying a snake had bitten her.

The bottom part of the cow paddock was low lying and I had often seen snakes there. Most of them, I reckon, were tigers. I've always blamed myself for not warning her about those snakes. Anyway, I jumped out of bed and cut the fang marks in her leg and sucked the cut to get the poison out and rubbed condy's crystals in. I should have put a ligature on as well, but I never knew any better then.

There was a neighbour about two miles away who had a sulky, so I told Mrs Murphy to lie down while I went for help. I pushed the corner of a sack bag in to make a sort of cloak and ran all the way to his place. I was still in my pyjamas. It started raining like hell and by the time I got there I was as wet as a shag. We ran the sulky horse in, harnessed it and went flat as a strap back to Murphy's farm.

The neighbour bloke put a ligature on Mrs Murphy's leg,

then we wrapped her in a blanket and headed to the nearest town, about eight miles away. By the time we got there she was unconscious, and I was shivering like a dog passing razor blades. To cut a long story, she was put into the local hospital, and I went in, too, with pneumonia. They never told me how she got on, but when I was well enough to travel, I was sent back to the bloody orphanage.

I looked at my mate and had to ask the question. 'Do you think she died?'

Snowy thought for a while. 'I think she must have, although I don't know. You know, I often thought of going back to find out, but always decided it was better not to.'

'What sort of a reception did you get at the orphanage? . . .'

Well, they didn't exactly roll out the red carpet. I reckon they thought they had got rid of me at the Murphys, and I think they blamed me for things not working out there. They made it as hard as they could, but the three years away had given me a sense of right and wrong and I stood up for myself even more than I had before. At the end of two years I was fostered out again, and this time they made sure I wouldn't have an easy time.

A bloke from the orphanage escorted me to a farm out from Penrith. The owner was a Dutchman with a timid little wife and a mongrel son who was two years older than me. This Dutchman had his wife so terrified that she wouldn't say boo to a goose, but he and his son made my life a misery. Hans was the son's name. He would deliberately do something wrong, then tell his old man that I had done it. I reckon I could have held my own with Hans in a stoush, but if I offered him out, he would tell his old man and I'd get another flogging.

Well, I put up with the bastards for eighteen months, then I made plans to square things and clear out. I waited for the Dutchman's apples to ripen, then went into action. I got a sugar bag and, after dark, picked a dozen apples. The weather was warm, so I folded up one of the blankets off my bed and stuck that in the bag as well. I then planted the bag down the paddock, and went to bed knowing that the next day would be one I'd remember. As it turned out, I wasn't far off the mark.

I waited until Hans and I were walking back from school, and made sure that I was in the lead. About a hundred yards from the house I turned around and kicked him on the nuts. I then got stuck into him and gave him a bloody good hiding. I knew I'd be for it when he got home so I raced to the stables and got a chain spreader. It was nearly three foot long and as thick as your wrist. I planted it behind the corner of the building and prepared to cop the hiding I knew I was in for.

What I didn't expect was that the bastard would do his block completely. He roared at me to come over to him, and as soon as I was close enough, he punched me in the face, knocking out two teeth. But that was only the preliminaries. He then tied my hands up to a beam, tore my shirt off and got stuck into me with a riding crop.

I swore to myself that I wouldn't sing out, but before he had finished, the blood was dripping down my back and groans as big as wool bales were flying out of me. When he had finished he untied me and told me to put my shirt back on. I did what he told me to do, with him standing there in front of me panting from his exertions. Without saying a word I then kicked him where I had kicked his son and ran for the stables. As I ducked around the corner, I heard him roaring like a wounded bull. He came after me, as I knew he would, and I waited with the spreader held ready. As he turned the corner, I hit him on the side of the head. He went down on his knees and I swung the spreader with full force, landing a blow on the back of his skull. Then I tossed my weapon on top of him and lit out.

I picked up the bag I had planted and kept going as though the hounds of hell were on my heels. I must have run for about five miles, crossing a road after making sure no one was in sight. I pulled up in a patch of scrub to catch my breath, and the realisation of what I had done began to sink in. I thought I might have killed the bastard and I wondered if they passed the death sentence on twelve-year-old kids. After a while I decided I had better put a bit more distance between me and the crime scene. I ran on, and just on sundown came to a bigger road heading east and west. I followed it to the west, keeping off it and out of sight.

As it was starting to get dark it began to drizzle, and I kept my eyes open for a camp. I spotted this culvert in the road over a shallow gully and I reckoned if it didn't rain hard it would be a good dry camp.

I had cleared some rubbish and weeds away from one end of the culvert when I heard a noise inside. Being wary of snakes, I got a stick and poked it about. The stick touched something soft and I heard a whimper. I had brought a box of wax matches with me, so partly crawling into the culvert, I struck one, to find a half-grown pup grovelling in front of me. He looked as if he'd had a hard time, and he was obviously starving. I brought my gear in and settled down, with the pup making it plain that he was pleased to see me. I tried to eat an apple but found my mouth was too sore. I solved the problem by cutting the apple into small pieces with my pocketknife. I have never known a dog to eat apples, but this bloke got stuck into the core of the first one I had finished, so after that, I shared the fruit with him.

I also shared my blanket with the pup, and he went to sleep happily. I'm afraid that was more than I did – my back was bloody sore. I couldn't lie on my back and every time I moved, it was murder. When daylight broke I crawled out and started to travel alongside the road again. I thought if I kept going west long enough I might escape the hangman. The pup came along with me, delighted to have someone who cared about him. I could relate to that hound a bit – like me, he was an outcast.

About midday I went a bit further off the road and sat down behind a big spreading bush. I had just started to cut up an apple, when I heard a motorbike coming. I lay doggo, but the pup gave the show away by racing out and barking. I heard the bike stop. I was hugging the ground, with the bloody pup licking my face, when I heard footsteps, then a gruff voice saying, 'Right, on your feet.'

I got up slowly and looked up into the face of a copper. He was a big man and a sergeant. He gave me the once over. 'Have you got any weapons on you?'

I looked at him stupidly, then stuttered, 'Only me pocketknife.'

'Let's have it, then,' he demanded, holding out his hand.

I handed it over. It wasn't much of a weapon, as it only had one blade. The other one was broken off at the handle. Anyway, he put it in his pocket and told me to empty out my bag.

'Leave the apples there,' he said. 'You won't need them where you're going – but bring the blanket.'

He then told me to walk ahead of him out to the road. When we got to the bike, he told me to get on the back and not to try any funny business.

'What about me dog?' I said. I'd taken a bit of a shine to the pup, and at that moment he was the only friend I had in the world.

'All right,' he growled, 'but you'll have to carry him.'

I stuck the blanket on the pillion seat and got on with the young dog in my arms. About twenty minutes later we came to a small town and the copper pulled up at the police station. It was just a small building beside his house with a one-room lock up down the back. He looked me over again after we got off the motorcycle.

'Who hit you in the mouth?'

I just stood there and said nothing.

'OK, have it your way,' he said. 'Come on. I've got to lock you up until I find out what to do with you.'

We walked down to the jail with the half-grown pup frisking beside us. I asked him if I could have the pup in with me, and after a pause he nodded. He opened the door and stood aside. I hesitated at the entrance and he gave me a push in the back. I flinched like a bad horse when he first feels the saddle.

'What's wrong with your back?'

I said nothing. Just stood there as I had done before.

'Come here and take your shirt off.'

I still didn't move.

'You heard me. Do it.'

It wasn't hard to remove the shirt. The buttons were gone and one sleeve was almost torn off, thanks to the Dutchman. Just the same, I took it off gingerly, as the bloody thing was stuck to my back in places. As soon as I had it off, he told me to turn around.

'Jesus wept,' he said, 'who did this to you?' Without waiting for an answer, he said, 'Come on over to the house. I'll get the missus to see what she can do with your back.'

We walked over to the house and went in the back door. A plump woman with a pleasant sorta face was standing at the kitchen sink.

'Have a look at this lad's back, love,' he says.

She dried her hands and came over. 'You mean his mouth, don't you?'

'No, his back – turn around,' he told me.

I did so and she gave a funny little cry. Next thing I knew she had turned me round to face her and I was in her arms.

'Oh, you poor child,' she kept saying. It was right out of the blue. Over the years I had built up this tough shield, to protect my feelings, but all at once it collapsed like a house of cards, and I'm buggered if I didn't start to bawl. I covered it up pretty quick, though. I pulled away, wiped the back of my hand across my eyes and muttered something about my back hurting. The copper, who had gone over to the tap for a drink of water, left the room with a funny look on his face.

The copper's wife took me into a bedroom and told me to lie face down on the bed. She went away and came back with a first aid box. She must have spent half an hour patching me up, then she gave me an aspirin and told me to get some sleep.

I didn't wake up until nearly dark. The policeman's missus

must have been keeping an eye on me, for soon after I surfaced she came in with a huge bowl of soup. She said she'd cooled it down so it wouldn't hurt my mouth. I mumbled thanks, and found I was bloody hungry. Fortunately the soup had plenty of solids in it and filled me up. I put the bowl on a small side table and lay back wondering what was going to happen to me next. Unexpected kindness can be disturbing, and I was totally confused. I had expected to be thrown in jail and perhaps even hung, and here I was being nursed in a soft bed.

Later that evening I had to go to the toilet. I slipped out and on my way back heard them talking in the kitchen.

'You aren't going to send him back to that brute, are you?' I heard her say.

'Not if I can help it. He's coming in tomorrow morning and I'll have a better idea of what happened when I question him.'

'If he doesn't go back there, what will we do with him?'

'It will be up to the Children's Services, I'm afraid. It's really out of our hands.'

I crept back to bed. So I didn't kill the big bastard, after all, I thought. The threat of the hangman evaporated, to be replaced by dismay at the thought of returning to the blasted orphanage, but at least that was better than jail.

I woke up early next morning. The missus came into the room and said she had run a bath for me. She gave me a towel and told me to be careful not to wet the dressing on my back. In the bathroom I found a new set of clothes set out for me. I was staggered by my change of luck, but knew it was too good to last. I wallowed in the bath tub and decided I would make the most of things while I had the chance.

I had breakfast with the copper and his wife, and managed a few words of thanks for the new outfit. If you're not used to that type of thing, it comes a bit hard. The sergeant told me what I already knew about the visit of the Dutchman, and added that he would be ringing the Children's Services later to put them in the picture.

I looked up from my plate. 'I'm pleased I didn't kill him.'

'You can count yourself lucky, too,' the copper said. 'Your friend the Dutchman must have a thick skull.'

From my bedroom window I saw the Dutchman arrive in his sulky. His head was bandaged, but otherwise he seemed pretty much the same. He went over to the little police station, but wasn't there for long. When he came out, he jumped in the sulky and drove away at high speed, giving the sulky horse hell. The copper's wife told me later that her husband had sent him away with a flea in his ear. She seemed very pleased about that.

I lived the life of Riley at the copper's place for three days, then an official from the Department came and took me back to the orphanage. Both the copper and his wife came to see me off at the railway station. They had promised to find a good home for the half-grown pup and I felt good about that. The policeman shook my hand and wished me luck. His missus planted a kiss on me and told me to write. I never did, of course.

I looked at Snowy. 'Why not?'

He thought about that for a moment, then said, 'Well, she was a nice person, but the bastards at the orphanage read all our letters before they went out. I would have been embarrassed to have those bludgers read what I would have written.'

'How long did you stay there that time? . . .'

I suffered it for another eight months, all the time planning to escape from the bloody place, I was over twelve years of age and I knew the chances of being fostered out at that age were slim. So I reckoned my only chance was to do a bunk. At the end of the year they used to take us out to Bondi Beach on New Year's Day. I decided I would do a bolt from there. The thought of that planned escape kept my chin up.

There were some odd bastards at that orphanage, I can tell you. We all slept in big dormitories, big and little kids in together. Some nights a couple of the blokes – teachers and other staff – would come in and take some of the little kids away. We were envious of those little tykes – we reckoned they were getting special privileges.

Knowing what I know now, and looking back on it, I don't think we had much to be jealous about. God knows what the poor little sods had to go through.

Anyway, the big day came. I slipped out of bed early and put two sets of clothes on without anyone noticing and took my pocketknife out of its hiding place. The policeman had returned it to me before I left Penrith and I had managed to keep it planted. At breakfast I got hold of the pepper pot and managed to get some pepper into a pocket. I had to work fast and a bit of pepper got up my nose. This was all to the good, as I had to pretend I had a cold to avoid the planned swim at the beach. I sneezed loudly and a few heads turned. Great, I thought.

We went to Bondi on the famous tram. I hoped to equal its well known speed in my escape. From the tram stop we walked to the beach. Every now and again I would put my hand in my pocket, rub my nose and sneeze like hell. We mucked around for a while, then had a lunch of sandwiches. I would grab a sandwich, take a bite and wander off, stuffing it in a pocket. By doing this, I finished up with four half-eaten sandwiches hidden away. As it was said to be dangerous to swim on a full stomach, we all sat around and sang songs for an hour. Each song was punctuated by my violent sneezing, and I was forbidden to enter the water.

With the kids in the water, the attention of the staff was on them. I approached a teacher and asked if I could go to the toilet. He nodded and told me to come straight back. The position of this toilet block was important to my plan. It was back off the sand, with the entrance on the side and hidden from the beach. As soon as I left, the teacher turned his attention back to the swimmers. I ran to the toilet block, then around the corner and kept going, keeping the toilet between me and the group on the beach. Being a holiday, the trams were fairly regular, but as it turned out I had to wait a while for one to arrive. It was probably only a few minutes, but it felt like hours. I jumped on board as far away from the tram conductor as I could. He finally arrived clicking his pinchers and calling 'Tickets please.'

I had a story ready, of course. I told him I had lost my money at the beach – I was meeting my mother in the city and she would fix him up. I nearly pulled it off. He hesitated, then told me I would have to get off at the next stop.

At the next stop there was a lot of people getting on and off. I got up and moved towards the door, then sat down. It was two stops before the conductor spotted me. At the next stop he put me off the tram himself. I wasn't worried, I had travelled five stops from the beach, and by pulling the same trick I finally got to the city. I knew they would look for me at Central railway station, but calculated on getting there before the word went out.

Without a ticket I had to plan my entry to the platform. I waited until a large woman came along with six tired and whingeing kids. I watched her buy tickets for her brood and as they followed her to the platform gate I tagged on behind. She shoved a handful of tickets at the railway man and we all trooped through. I grinned at him as I passed and said thanks sir.

Once on the platform, I asked a porter what time the next mail train left. I had three hours to wait, so picking up a newspaper from a seat, I planted in a toilet cubicle for the duration. I spent the time reading and dozing.

The departure of a mail train is unmistakable. I waited until the 'All seats please' call, then walked out and followed a group into a carriage in front of the toilet. Once on the train, I went to ground in the toilet at the end of the carriage. I don't know what the hell I would have done without those toilets. When we got well away from the station I came out and grabbed a seat. I found it pretty easy to dodge the conductor by moving around and occasionally ducking into the nearest toilet. This was in 1927. Things were not the best, but the depression had not yet hit and there wasn't a lot of blokes jumping the rattler.

I wasn't sure what train I had caught, but it turned out to be the Northern Mail. I sat back and considered my situation. First thing I would have to do was to change my name.

I had no idea what my first name really was – I'd always been Snowy, and I reckoned I'd have to stick with that. I hated my surname; it was all the bastards at the orphanage ever called me. It was, 'Barrett, do this', and 'Barrett, do that'; 'Barrett, stand up straight'. I reckoned I'd be well rid of it. In the newspaper I had been reading was an article on the national leaders during the Great War, blokes like Billy Hughes and the rest of them. It gave a big wrap to an American called Wilson. I've forgotten his first name, but I liked the sound of Wilson. That will do me, I thought, and I've been Snowy Wilson ever since.

Snowy stood up and stretched. 'Well, Simmo, enough of my sordid past; we'd better strike a blow. I reckon the missus has had her beauty sleep by now.'

The cloud cover had increased and a few drops of rain were falling when we began on the roof of the back verandah. The cyclone, though obviously still a long way off, had not only landed us the job but was now making the task reasonably comfortable. We discarded the carpet runners as not only unnecessary but a brake on our progress. Light rain fell during the afternoon without interrupting our work on the verandah.

By five o'clock we were finished, and started on the hotel's main roof. The pitch was quite steep and we found working on it far more difficult than on the other areas. To make matters worse, the rain had made the galvanised iron quite slippery. We were forced to hang on tooth and nail as we worked our way up towards the ridge capping. Snowy looked down at me. 'Bloody hell, a man needs to be a cross between a flying fox and a telegraph pole to do this job.'

I laughed. 'Well, boss, it was your brilliant idea. You'll have to stick to it, but I reckon I'd feel more secure with a bloody parachute.'

We were saved from our slippery situation by the dinner bell. We climbed stiffly down the ladder and headed for the laundry for a wash.

'I'm just about knackered,' Snowy groaned. 'I'm going to have a rum.'

I agreed. With the weather having cooled off, it was a good night for a rum, I added.

'Since when did the weather have anything to do with drinking rum,' Snow snorted. 'Come on, we've got time for a couple before we eat.'

I followed my mate into the bar and ordered rums from the barmaid. We were conscious of the publican's scrutiny, but we had put in a big day and we knew a few rums wouldn't break him. We got another rum into us, then made our way to the dining room, feeling a lot better. Maisie greeted us like we were long lost brothers and handed us an impressive-looking menu. We had an excellent meal and when I had finished my dessert I looked at Snowy and said, 'Well, mate, the cook is making sure she will be missed. Cooking like that is going to be a hard act to follow.'

Snow nodded. 'Yes, there's no doubt she can cook when she wants to. But have no fear, I was taught by a man who had cooked for the Prince of Wales ... and other bush hotels,' he added.

As Maisie picked up our plates, Snowy continued. 'Yes, when I'm in the kitchen, I'll have Maisie here so fat her mother won't know her.'

Maisie gave him a sharp look. 'Just as long as it's only caused by your cooking,' she quipped, and returned to the kitchen.

We sat back in our chairs, replete and at peace with the world.

'Come on,' said Snowy, 'let's go for a walk and get the kinks out of our legs.'

It wasn't a bad idea. We strolled down the little main street, looking in the few shop windows. There wasn't a lot to see, and we returned to the pub for a night cap. The barmaid, Joan, was serving the few locals. We ordered rum, gave her a bit of cheek for a while, then sought our swags.

# 4

We walked out onto the back verandah and stretched out on our bunks. Crawling around on a roof brings out aches and pains in muscles you never knew you had. Snowy rolled a smoke, and when he had it going to his satisfaction, he turned his head and inquired if I was sleepy. Knowing he was really asking if I wanted to hear more of his experiences in the Great Depression, I said, 'No, mate. Tell me, did you manage to get away from the orphanage?'

Snowy took a drag on his smoke and got into his stride.

Well, you know I was on that train. I reckoned the cops might be watching every station, so I always planted when the train stopped. I finally slipped off the rattler at Maitland. It was still as dark as a dog's guts, so I looked around the place to see what I could find. Behind a produce store I grabbed a couple of feed bags and headed down to the river. On the way down I picked up a rope clothes line from behind a house. God knows what the woman of the house thought when she came to peg out her next wash. I passed a rubbish dump a bit further on, and I rooted around there for a bit and found a big treacle tin that hadn't long been empty. I also found a board with a nail stuck in it, and a piece of tie wire. With my gathered loot, I headed for the river. I followed it upstream and out of town a bit until I found a good camp with plenty of cover.

Splitting the bags with my old pocketknife, I made two Wagga rugs, or bush blankets. I then got to work and cleaned the tin out. I put two holes in the top with the nail, and with a tie wire handle I had a first rate billy. Satisfied with my work, I settled down to get a bit of sleep.

It was broad daylight when I woke up. I took off the spare set of clothes and rolled them up in the bag blankets. With two bits of rope around it, I had a swag. I shouldered the thing and continued up the river. I found out by road signs that it was the Hunter. There was plenty of fruit about, so I didn't go hungry.

On the second day I started calling on farms, looking for work. I was big for my age and as fit as a fiddle, and the third day I landed a farm job at seven and six a week, with keep. Thanks to being fostered out, I had no trouble doing the work. At last I was a free agent, with money in my pocket. The farmer must have wondered about me a bit. I wouldn't go into town – if I wanted anything, I got him to get it for me. One day he tried to pump me about my past.

I told him nothing and at the end of the week I pulled out and went further up the Hunter Valley. I worked on farms there for the next two years, getting ten bob a week towards the end. I had no idea what I should have been paid, but I was happy – I was getting money for work I had done for nothing for nearly four years. Things were getting tough by then and the farmers were getting very little for their crops. A lot of the farms were old established places. Some had blocks taken off them, but all seemed to be into the banks.

I pulled on any work I could get: I picked grapes, did ringbarking, a bit of fencing, and became pretty handy with team horses. The working conditions on the farms were usually pretty good. The tucker was plain, but they always fed you well. On a lot of the places I worked, I ate with the family. I usually slept in one of the farm outbuildings. A couple of times when I was doing seasonal work, I dossed in a tent.

Anyway, early in twenty-nine I moved on. I reckoned I'd try my hand at timber cutting, but I soon found out that there was a lot of trouble in that industry too. There were strikes in Victoria and these were spreading to New South Wales. I gave up the idea of swinging an axe and headed out to Tamworth to try my luck. By this time I was pretty well set up, with a good solid swag and camp gear. I was nearly fifteen and bloody pleased with myself, I can tell you. The threat of the orphanage had all but disappeared and I was holding my own in a man's world. At Tamworth I camped on the river, and was not surprised to find unemployed men camped there as well. I kept to myself but often overheard them talking.

I was surprised just how well informed they were, but I suppose you soon learn about a situation that has thrown you on the scrap heap. There was never any agreement among them, though, about how the problem should be solved. Most of them criticised the Bruce Government, and some of them talked about a bloke called Scullin and another named Theodore. Talk about a character they called the 'Big Fella' always stirred the possum in the camp. A few reckoned he was a 'commo', but they were always shouted down with cries of: 'What about the widows' pension. What about child endowment? And what about workers' compo.' It was all bloody confusing to me, I can tell you, but I gathered that the country was in a mess and likely to get worse.

Every day I walked up town and did the rounds of the business houses looking for odd jobs. I picked up a few bob that way and often got a bit of tucker instead of money. After a week I decided to try my luck in a smaller place and I carried my swag up to Manilla. I was there for only a couple of days, when my luck changed. I was camped a few miles out of town on the banks of the Namoi, but walked up town each day. One morning about ten o'clock, I was standing on a street corner when a horsey-looking chap came up to me and asked me if I was looking for a job. I said my bloody oath I was.

He looked me over. 'It's a droving job. Can you ride?'

'Yeah,' I said, 'I can ride a bit.'

'Right, I've got a mob of cows and calves to take on the road for sale. I can give you a quid a week and tucker.'

I said that would do me. He told me to pick up my gear and gave me directions to get to his house on the edge of town. I was to wait there for him. When I got to the house, it was really only a five by ten yard shed. There were seven rough-looking horses in the fenced allotment and a spring cart.

I threw my gear down by the cart at the back of the house and looked the horses over. As I turned away, a woman poked her head out of the open back door and asked me in for a cup of tea. The house was pretty crude; there were bags laid down over a dirt floor, and the shed was divided into two rooms by a hessian curtain hung from a greenhide rope. The woman had done what she could to make the place presentable. There were pictures cut from magazines and papers pasted on the walls, and I noticed that she and her two little kids were spotless. There was no stove in the living area of the shed – the cooking was done in a galley out the back.

I've noticed that all women in poor circumstances are compelled to explain the reason for their position. The drover's wife was no different. She told me her husband had been a stockman in Queensland when she married him. They had moved to Sydney then, in hope of a better life, and had bought a small house at Bankstown. Her husband got a job in a sawmill and everything seemed rosy. Then when the strikes hit the timber industry, they sold the house at a loss and moved to Tamworth. She assured me that Tom, her husband, would soon be on his feet again. I noticed that the only light on the rough table was a fat lamp, a container of lard with a cloth wick stuck in it. I sort of made sympathetic noises and escaped as soon as I could.

Anyway, this Tom arrived soon after with another young chap who said his name was Bill and an Aborigine, called Joe Brown, who looked about thirty. After a few minutes Tom came out with a billy of black tea and a large plate of damper and treacle.

Joe Brown grinned. 'Get it into you, lads, and sleep on beef bags. You won't get fat this trip.'

Joe turned out to be a real character who saw humour in just about everything. He was quick to laugh and wasn't at all sensitive about his colour. He was a good man in a camp, and was always ready to give a hand. When we had finished the damper and tea, Bill and Joe rolled smokes and we sat back to await developments.

After a little while Tom came out and told us we could shoe the horses. He added that he had to go up town again to see the agents, and that we could find the shoeing tools in the spring cart and a bag of slippers underneath it. I had been around horses long enough to know that slippers were horseshoes that had some use but had been pulled off before becoming worn out. Having been fitted previously, they needed little shaping, making the job a lot easier.

Although I had done little shoeing before, with Joe's help I managed to put the slippers on one of the horses. I looked up, pleased with my efforts, to find that Bill was struggling with his second horse while Joe had finished his third. Joe caught the last horse and led it over to inspect my work.

'You better tighten them clinches,' he said. 'The boss can't afford new shoes, so we'd better get as many miles as we can out of these slippers.'

He showed me how to hold the pinchers under the ends of the nails as he hit the nail heads with the shoeing hammer. 'Always keep the clinches short,' he added. 'That way, the shoes will wear out before they ever become loose.'

He started on the horse he had caught and I watched with interest as he went about the job. He worked with a series of smooth actions and a minimum of effort. I decided there and then that Joe Brown was a man I could learn a lot from. In the meantime, Bill, with a string of curses, had finished the horse he had been shoeing, and was complaining about the shoeing gear. I didn't say anything, but thought of the old saying that a poor tradesman blames his tools.

When the shoeing job was done, the drover's wife brought out a billy of tea and some slices of brownie. Once we had finished smoko, Joe Brown looked at Bill and me. 'If the boss isn't back soon, I think we should get these horses a drink and hobble them out on feed.'

'Do you?' said Bill. 'You do what you like, but I don't take orders from blackfellas.'

Joe didn't say anything. I got up. 'Come on,' I said. 'I'll give you a hand.'

As I saddled one of the horses, I heard Bill mutter something about white blackfellas. I knew then that as sure as there was dung in a goose he and I would clash before the trip was over. The prospect didn't daunt me at all. I had as many fights as feeds at the orphanage and I had surprised a few blokes along the Hunter who had made the mistake of under-estimating me because of my age. Bill was taller and older than me, but I reckoned I could handle him if I had to.

Joe and I were just letting the horses out of the gate when Tom arrived. Joe mounted his horse and rode over to him. They talked for a while, then Joe returned and told me that Tom wanted the horses tailed on grass until sundown, then brought back to the allotment. We watered the horses, then took them out to a hollow where there was good green pick.

I've got to admit that I was intrigued by this Joe Brown. You see, I had never had anything to do with Aborigines before this. I pumped him about his past, and it was obvious he didn't mind talking about it. He said he came from a place called Clermont in Queensland. He had come down into New South Wales with a drover a few years before and had worked there ever since. With a broad grin, he told me that if things didn't improve soon he would be going back to bloody Clermont.

He told me about wild cattle and scrub dashing. He talked of throwing cleanskin bulls and of riding buckjumpers. I lapped it all up, although, for all I knew, he could have been having me on. On our return to the house, I noticed some cooking gear and rations had been loaded into the spring cart.

Later, out at our swags, we had a meal of damper and corned beef. After we had finished, Tom came out and told us his plans. We would be leaving at daylight next morning to go out to the station and pick up the mob. The place was about fifteen miles south-west, so it would take a day to get there. He went on to tell us that the mob was being put on the road for sale due to drought conditions. The spring cart would double as ration cart and calf cart.

Seeing my bemused look, he informed me that the cart would pick up calves that had knocked up. He added that it would also carry newborn calves until they were strong enough to travel. Tom then advised us of our jobs. He and Joe would be with the mob, while Bill and I would take half-day turns at driving the cart and being with the cattle. Then he informed us that he would do whatever cooking there was to be done.

These arrangements did not seem to please Bill. He didn't say anything, but apparently regarded himself as boss drover material. To me, the whole thing was a new experience, I was going droving. I crawled into my swag as happy as a dog with two tails.

After a quick snack next morning, we got organised. Tom put a solid bay horse called Boozer in the spring cart, and told me I could drive the cart while he and the others took the spare horses along. I dare say he wanted to see if I could handle the job. It was child's play to me, as I'd done a lot of team work on the Hunter. The day passed without trouble and we camped where the cows and calves were being held. Next morning Tom took delivery of the mob. A lot of the cows were in poor condition, with calves hanging on them. There were also many heavy in calf.

We started off with me driving the spring cart and the other three driving the three spare horses along with the cattle.

I looked over at my mate. 'It seems like a bloody rough droving plant.'

Snowy nodded.

It was, but then I knew no different. It wasn't until later I realised what a cock-rag turnout it was. Anyway, I was happy I was going droving, like Clancy of the Overflow. You see, I had picked up a book of Paterson's poems in Tamworth. I reckoned the world was my oyster. As the days passed, I realised that droving cows and calves is a bastard of a game. Some of the calves that couldn't travel were bloody heavy.

They had to be heaved into the calf cart and often tied down. Most of the time you got covered with calf dung and smelt like a night cart. Bill didn't like this part of the job at all. He whinged all the time about it, and I dare say he had a point. The only good thing about that mob was no night watching – we were in lanes most of the time, and just camped behind the cows.

Joe came over to me one day when I was with the mob and gave me his opinion of cows and calves.

'You know,' he said, 'if I owned this mob, I'd knock every bloody calf on the head. That way, you may save the cows.'

It wasn't until later on in the trip that I realised how right he was.

Bill was still having the occasional dig at me, but I was prepared to bide my time. A fortnight into the trip an Afghan hawker pulled up as we got to the night camp. He had two very poor horses pulling a van. Unyoking the horses, he opened the sides of the vehicle to display his wares. I bought a pair of moleskin riding trousers, a cheap redhide whip and a pair of Koriella riding boots. I reckoned that gear was the duck's guts. Tom paid the hawker for the stuff everyone bought and told us he would deduct it later from our cheques.

Bill's dislike of me came to a head on dinner camp one day. Tom had ridden ahead to try and find feed for the mob. I had driven the cursed calf cart that morning and when Joe started the mob up, I walked over to the horse Bill had been riding.

'Get away from my horse, you young bastard,' Bill snarled. 'You can drive the cart this afternoon.'

'Well, Bill,' I said, 'you can get f...ed.'

I knew it would be on, and I wasn't wrong. He raced at me, cursing. I'm sure he thought I would dingo. When I walked to meet him, he propped and shaped up. He danced around me for a while, landing a few long range punches. I thought to myself, this bastard can't hit hard and closed with him. I took a bit of punishment, but once I got close, I doubled him up with a couple to the guts, then stepped back and flattened him with a haymaker to the jaw. To his credit he got up, but I was waiting for him and laid him out again. I was standing over Bill to see if he was going to try again, when Joe rode over.

'That's enough, Snowy. Hop on your horse and block up the lead while I get the tail moving.'

It was good advice and I took it. We got to the night camp without any further action.

Tom met us there. He looked hard at Bill, but asked no questions. At breakfast next morning, Bill rolled his swag and came over to where we were sitting.

'I'll finish up at the next town we come to,' he told Tom.

'Oh, will you?' said Tom. 'Well, if you're going to pull out, you can do it at my bloody pleasure, not yours. Take your bloody swag out to the road now. You're finished.'

This was not the response Bill had been expecting.

'What about the money you owe me?' he whined.

Tom told him that with the tobacco he had got and the hawker's bill, they were square. I had me doubts about that, but there was nothing Bill could do about it. The last time I saw him, he was sitting on his swag by the road. I dare say he got a lift from someone. Of course, I had to drive the blasted calf cart until Tom got another man, and I began to regret ever being goaded by Bill.

At the end of six weeks I'd had a gutful of droving. I reckoned I'd stick it out, though. My opinion of Clancy of the Overflow also changed. Instead of a romantic hero, I regarded him as a bloody dickhead.

We began to lose cows, and Joe's remarks about killing the calves started to make sense. Of course, it wasn't up to Tom. He was only the drover. Cows became bogged at watering places, some just got too weak to travel and others started to slip stillborn calves. I suppose that was nature's way of saving the cows. We were only managing to go five or six miles a day, and although a couple of agents had inspected the mob, the cows had not been sold.

The cows were finally sold over the Victorian border, near Swan Hill. I'm not sure how long we were on the road with them – I sorta lost track of time – but it was over three months. Joe was staying with Tom to give him a hand to take the plant back. Tom gave me my cheque and I got a ride into Swan Hill with the stock and station agent. As soon as I got to town, I went to a bank and asked the teller to cash the cheque.

I've always had a snout on tellers due to that bastard. He looked down his nose at me and told me the cheque was on a different bank and in New South Wales. I could open an account if I wished, but it would take a week for the cheque to clear. Those days you could open an account without worrying about identification.

Anyway, I did what he said and opened a bloody account, then waited for my money at my camp on the river. I had a few bob left and I got by all right. At the end of the week, I went back to the bank. The teller grinned when he saw me and told me the cheque had bounced. The bastard seemed to think it was a joke. I resisted the urge to job him and walked out. Bloody hell, I thought, I went through all that bastardry on the road for a dud cheque. I did have a pair of boots and the other gear from the hawker, so I tried to look on the bright side. I managed to survive until I got a job cutting scrub for a bloke's sheep for ten bob a week and tucker.

Snowy stopped to roll a smoke and I interrupted his story.

'Mate, it seems to me that you were adopting an "f... you, Jack, I'm OK" attitude when it came to getting a job.'

He thought for a minute ...

Well, you're right, of course, but you've got to remember I was a loner. I'd survived by looking after number one and letting the world look after its bloody self. Old Chilla had a lot to say about unity and mateship after I started knocking around with him. But at times when things got real hard, I've seen Chilla disgusted with his fellow workers.

Anyway, I took the job. Jack was the bloke's name. I'm not

sure if the place he had was a soldier settler's block or not, but it was a starvation joint, in my opinion. The poor bastard's sheep were in a bad way. He had a brother working for him who gave me a hand as well, although I don't know if he was ever paid.

This brother – his name was Arthur – had been made stone deaf in the war and apparently had been buried by a shell for some time before he was dug out. This poor bastard hardly ever spoke, just grunted. He would freeze at times, no matter what he was doing, and stand like a statue for up to five minutes. To put it crudely, I don't think the poor sod knew if he was Arthur or Martha. He and I shared a lean-to shed, and the noises he made at night used to make the hairs stand up on the back of my neck. I never really got used to it, although I never let on it bothered me.

On a Sunday afternoon after I had been there three weeks I was in the lean-to sewing a button back on the fly of one of my strides. Arthur, the deaf bloke, was staring straight ahead, and I reckon what he was seeing wasn't of this world. Jack, who owned the farm, came in and sat down on the end of my bunk and told me he couldn't afford to keep me on any longer. He said the bank had cut off his credit and if things didn't improve there was a chance the bank would sell him up. He was bitter about it, too. Jack said he and two brothers had gone to the war, and he wondered now what the hell they had been fighting for. He said his younger brother had been killed in France, and Arthur – Jack stopped and rolled a smoke.

Jack lit the cigarette and nodded towards his brother. 'You wouldn't think so now, but Arthur was one of the best athletes in the district before the war. He gave up the chance to play football in Melbourne and enlisted with Kevin and me. I've got a wife and kids to worry about. Christ knows what will happen to him if I lose this place.'

At the orphanage, they had filled us with all that patriotic flag-waving bullshit about the British Empire. Every morning we were paraded; we would salute the flag and sing God save the King. When I left Jack's run, it was with a different outlook on the Great War.

I rolled the swag next day and departed. Before I left, Jack gave me a cheque and assured me that the bank would honour it. I walked out to the main road and headed east. I hadn't gone half a mile when a commercial traveller picked me up. It was rather strange, for blokes in cars didn't usually pick up swagmen. Perhaps he took pity on me, or just wanted someone to talk to. He certainly had the gift of the gab. He said he was going to Echuca, and I said that was fine with me. He then brought me up to date with what had been happening in Australia and overseas. The Federal Government had been defeated. I gathered the defeated prime minister had lost the support of his own party when he tried to sack some sort of court. Scullin and Theodore should fix things up, he reckoned – although, he added darkly, there had been a financial crash in America and a lot of financial high fliers in the States were jumping out of skyscrapers without parachutes. I said I didn't see how this would affect us, but he told me the depression was going to be worldwide.

This bloke was a Rawlings traveller with a Ford van. I'd never been in a motor car before, and made up my mind that I would buy a car one day. I haven't got around to it yet, but, you'll see, I will. Anyway, when we got to Echuca I asked this bloke if he'd mind dropping me off at the bank, and told him if I ran into him after I'd cashed my cheque I would buy something from him. He pulled up outside the bank and I hopped out and went in. I handed the cheque to the teller, who looked at it and took it out the back.

Here we go again, I thought, but he came back and gave me the money without a word.

Sales must have been bloody bad, for the Rawlings bloke was waiting for me at the kerb. I bought some corn cure from him, thanked him again and headed for the river. There were mobs of unemployed blokes camping there. Blind Freddy could see that things were getting crook.

I hung around Echuca for a couple of weeks, then decided I'd seen enough of Victoria. I crossed the Murray and carried my swag into New South Wales. Wherever I went, it was the same story – there was no work. I found even the odd jobs had dried up in the towns I went through. I reckon the school kids were helping out their families. I camped on the Murrumbidgee at Hay for a while and caught a few rabbits with an old trap I had found. I got by all right, although my money was almost gone.

I went up town this Saturday morning to get a few rations. I reckoned I had enough cash left to buy tea, flour and cream of tartar and soda. On the way to the shops, I had to pass the picture show. I glanced at the posters outside and saw it was a Tom Mix picture. I'd heard Joe and Bill talk of this Tom Mix character – apparently he was a pretty smart man with a horse. I hung around the entrance of the theatre, reading all the publicity on the show. You've got no idea how much I wanted to see that picture. I counted the change in my pocket again, in the hope that I had made a mistake. But I had to face facts and, dragging my feet a bit, I went to the bloody shops and bought what I had to. I had one bloody penny left, but I stopped at the picture show again on the way back. I saw there was a matinee on at three that afternoon, children's tickets sixpence.

I cursed the depression and headed back to camp. I had not gone twenty yards when I saw it in the gutter – a flaming sixpence. I swooped on it like a copper on a cold beer, then, clutching the coin in my hand, I went back and double checked at the picture show.

Sixpence for children under fourteen, the notice said. I realised I still had a problem. I was over fifteen and a big lump of a lad. I had one thing going for me, though. Because of my colouring, I had a very light beard and did not have to shave often. I decided to try and bluff my way in. I had nothing to lose: if I failed, I'd still have my sixpence.

I hurried back to camp and washed an old pair of shorts and a long sleeved shirt. While they were drying, I had a swim and shaved the bum fluff off my face. At half past two I went up to the picture show. I was in bare feet to reduce my height, and waited for the right time to join the queue.

After a little while, a large lady with two big kids came and stood at the end of the line. I took my chance and tagged on behind her. Fortune favoured the brave, I suppose, because two blokes who looked like shearers lined up behind me. The ticket window was fairly high, so I slumped my shoulders and approached it with a bent-kneed walk, like Groucho Marx. I'd never seen the Marx brothers at that time, but whenever I saw them later I remembered Tom Mix. Anyway, I slid over the sixpence and the woman gave me a ticket without even looking at me. I waited until the lights went out in the theatre, then walked up to the girl at the door in the same bent-kneed manner. She probably thought I was a polio victim. I found a seat and sat back to enjoy the show. It was the first time I had ever seen a picture.

I moved on, carrying my swag up the river, then went to Griffith. My sandshoes more or less fell off my feet and I had to foot slog it in my riding boots. They are bastards of things to walk in and I was pleased I had bought that corn cure from the Rawlings traveller. I spent Christmas at Griffith – and that was all I did spend. I was broke. I trapped a few bunnies and hawked them door to door. You could get a bob a head for rabbits then, but everyone was doing it. Most of the bludgers I caught I had to eat myself. I realised that despite the change of government, things were going to get worse. I reckoned I'd be able to survive, though.

'Anyway, we'd better get some shut eye. I'll finish the yarn some other time.'

# 5

When we woke up next morning, the cloud was lifting. It looked as if the cyclone was not going to give the district the much-needed rain everyone was waiting for. Before breakfast Snowy led the way onto the main roof. We had made little progress the evening before, but now with the weather clearing I thought the job would be a bit easier. Snowy made a great show of our early start, to the chagrin of a commercial traveller who had been enjoying a sleep in. He came out in a dressing gown, waving his arms in protest. He got short shrift from Snowy, who told him to go and perform an act that was not only obscene but physically impossible. I noticed that my mate was making a lot of noise to little effect. I said nothing, no doubt Snowy was thinking ahead.

When the breakfast bell rang, we had a clean up, then strolled into the dining room and sat in our usual places. Maisie was in high spirits and talked to us for a while after she had taken our order. The unfortunate commercial traveller, having sampled Snowy's wit once, waited patiently. We had a leisurely breakfast, and after the room cleared, Snowy gave me the drum.

'Look, Simmo, we've got to make this job last. The cyclone's gone, so there's no hurry. I've got the cooking, but you've got to get another day out of it at least.'

I nodded agreement and we returned to the roof. Working at half pace, we had completed about a quarter of the area by lunch. I noticed my mate was limping after we had climbed down the ladder. Knowing Snowy, I realised it was part of his devious plan. This assumption was proved correct when after the meal he limped into the bar and advised the publican he would be unable to work on the roof because of a sprained ankle. He assured the publican that with a day's spell he'd be able to handle the cooking. Snowy liked to cover all the angles.

I worked away on the roof after lunch, and by the time the dinner bell went, I had the job half finished. The cook put on another gourmet meal, but Snowy wasn't in the least impressed. After dinner I reported my progress on the roof to Snowy. He looked at me sadly. 'Simmo, you must never work yourself out of a job. Here I am with a sprained ankle to give you a chance and you're working your guts out.'

I assured my mate that I wasn't working my guts out and that I'd get another day and a half out of the job. Mollified by my assertion, Snowy suggested a few drinks. The publican, who was perhaps wondering when his roof would be finished, came over.

Snowy assured him that if he hadn't done his ankle, the job would have been finished already. 'Just bad luck,' he said. 'But Simmo here will clean it up tomorrow . . . or perhaps the day after,' he added quickly. With that, mine host had to be content. He would know that Snow had him by the short and curlies. He would also have known that with meals and the odd rum or two the contract price was not as cheap as it had first appeared.

We retired to our bunks, well pleased with ourselves. My mate stretched out. 'You know, Old Chilla always said if you got one square meal a day and a bed at night, you were going all right.'

After an afternoon's bludge, my mate was obviously in fine form. He looked over at me. 'Have I ever told you about the time Chilla and me put it over that bookie?'

'No mate, you haven't, but what I'd like to know is how the pair of you met and became mates? . . .'

Well, you remember me telling you about being up in New South Wales at Griffith for Christmas. Well, I knocked around for a bit living on bloody stewed rabbit, with a bit of pigweed thrown in when I could get it. I was bloody broke and scared to go near the cops because of the orphanage business. I bludged a bit of tea and flour whenever I could, and I did a day's work here and there for tucker if it was offered. Things were going from bad to worse, some of the blokes I met were unhappy with the new Labor Government.

Anyway, I was sitting on the verandah of this pub in a town in western New South Wales. There were quite a few blokes there, shearers and station hands. They were all moaning about the bloody depression. With them was a bloke they called the town pug. He was a big, ugly bastard, about thirty, I reckon, and must have weighed thirteen stone. He had a few mates with him, real crawlers who laughed every time he had a shot at someone. Anyway, this freckle-faced kid came around the corner carrying a paper bag. The publican had a side window where he served under-aged drinkers and Aborigines. The kid was nine or ten years old, he had bare feet and was dressed in hand-me-down clothes. The pug thought he'd have a bit of fun with the kid. He stepped onto the footpath and bailed him up.

'What have you got in the bag, boy?'

'It's beer for me old man,' said the kid.

'Why doesn't your old man get his own beer? What is he, a scab?'

'Me old man ain't no scab, he's crook.'

'Well, let's see what sort of medicine you've got for him,' laughs the pug, and grabs the bag. The kid pulls back on it and the bag splits open and three bottles of beer smash onto the footpath.

The kid was only knee-high to a grasshopper, but he ripped into the big bastard.

'Look what you've gone and done, you stinking big mongrel,' he yelled.

The town pug belts him one in the ear. 'Get home, you cheeky little bugger, and tell your old man you ran into Billy Smith.'

The pug's mates seemed to think the whole thing was a great joke. But I couldn't help myself, I flew up and got stuck into the big standover merchant. I reckon I held me own with him for five seconds, then he belted piss and pick handles out of me.

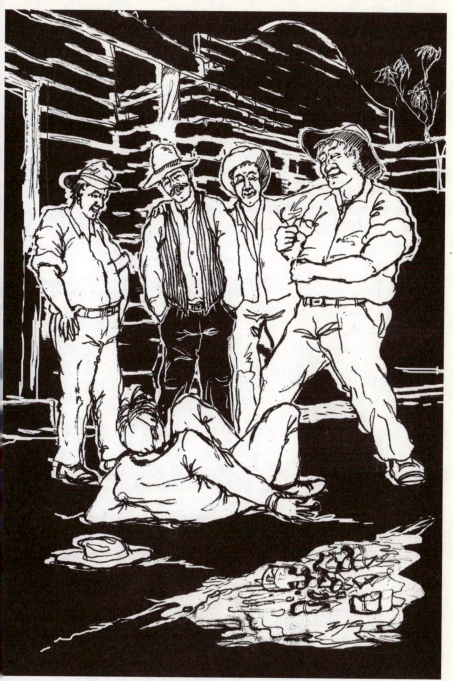

*I reckon I held me own with him for five seconds, then he belted piss and pick handles out of me.*

I was about to get up for a third time, when a bloke I hadn't noticed before stepped up beside the pug. He grabbed the pug's right wrist with his left hand and lifted it high above the pug's head.

'The winner,' he announced. 'The winner by a knockout.'

The pug tries to free his arm, but this bloke holds it up without effort – and, of course, he has his own right arm free.

'I'm scouting for a gym in Sydney,' he said, 'looking for talent to take back to the big smoke.' He looked at the pug. 'You throw a good hard punch, but I've got to find out if you can take punishment?'

With that, he drives his right fist into the pug's guts. The pug's knees buckle, and he would have gone down, only this bloke had him jacked up by the right arm.

'We need to do a bit of work on the old comic cuts,' he said. 'And we can't afford to spend money training chaps who have glass jaws.'

He slammed his fist into the side of the pug's jaw, the pug's eyes rolled back, and this time this bloke lets him go, and he folds up like a rag doll on the footpath.

'A pity that,' the bloke says, 'I thought he may have made the grade.'

He walked over to the kid, who had been watching the exhibition open mouthed.

'How much was the beer?' he asks the kid.

The kid swallowed hard. 'Three bob,' he told him.

This bloke went over to the pug – who was still out to it – and he goes through his pockets until he finds ten bob.

'Here you are,' he says to the kid. 'Get the beer for your dad, and buy your mother something with the change. Forget about Billy Smith, tell your dad you met Chilla O'Rourke.'

This Chilla bloke then walks over to where I'm sitting and looks me over.

'You'll live,' he grinned. 'Have a clean up and I'll buy you a drink.'

There was a tap at the end of the verandah, so I washed

the blood off me face and then walked into the bar. I'd never been in a bar before and was far too young to drink. I saw Chilla standing at the bar with two beers in front of him. He introduced himself and looked at me.

'I don't think you're old enough to have a beer, but the way your face looks, nobody is going to know the difference.'

I took a swig out of the glass – it tasted bloody awful. I straightened myself up. Those days I was full of youthful pride. 'I can take care of myself,' I told him, 'no one has to fight my battles.'

'Is that so?' he said. 'Well, I didn't step in to fight your battles. He could have killed you, for all I care. I bought into it because of what he did to the kid, and because you were too bloody useless to do anything about it. I don't mean to be unkind, but if you want to play the knight in shining armour, you have to be able to use your fists. Stepping in like you did may look noble, but it achieves nothing. My advice to you is this – learn to fight, or learn to walk away. If you don't, you'll be punch drunk before you're old enough to vote.'

That sat me back a bit, I can tell you. I had had a few wins and was beginning to think I was pretty good. I had another swig of beer and looked directly at him.

'Well, I thought I could fight a bit, but I'm not sixteen yet and that bastard was too big.'

'He wasn't only too big,' Chilla said, 'he was too good.'

'Yeah, but I couldn't walk away from that kind of stand-over merchant.'

Chilla thought for a while, then stuck out his hand. 'Well, I like your style, and you've got guts. If you're interested, I'll show you a point or two. Where are you camped?'

I told him my swag was up at the trucking yards.

'That's not a good camp. After you've finished your beer, pick your gear up and go down to the waterhole just south of the town. If anyone bails you up, just tell 'em I sent you.'

He took a long drink from his glass and looked at me. 'For Christ's sake, stop looking over your shoulder.'

I felt a bit of a fool. 'I thought that pug and some of his mates might come looking for us.'

'No, Snowy, at the moment he hasn't got any mates. He'll slink home like a mongrel dog and lick his wounds for a few days. Later his cronies will convince him that I only had a win by king-hitting him. They'll tell him that in a fair fight he'd be able to beat me easily. After a few days of hearing that kind of advice he'll want to fight me, but it won't be for a while.'

I finished my beer, and feeling slightly light headed, I went up to the railway yards and picked up my gear. I didn't have a great deal, mind you. Just a thin swag, a sugar bag with a few things in it, a billy can and a waterbag.

As I came to the waterhole Chilla told me about, a grey-haired bloke stood up and glared at me.

'This is a private camp,' he told me.

If I hadn't just copped a hiding I would have given him a bit of cheek. Instead I said that Chilla had sent me there, and that satisfied him. He nodded to a nearby tree.

'Well, that's his camp there,' he said, and returned to his swag.

I threw my swag and gear down where the geezer had indicated. Chilla had picked a top camp – the tree was a real chloroform job. I filled my waterbag up from the waterhole, then unrolled my swag. In a few minutes I was dead to the world.

I didn't wake up until Chilla nudged me gently in the ribs with a boot.

'How about stoking the fire up and putting the billy on, young Snowy.'

I got the fire going well, then put the billy on. I then asked him where the tea was. He took a long, hard look at me and said, 'Don't you have anything at all?'

I felt pretty small, I can tell you, and hung my head. I never had a bloody thing, you see, not even tea leaves.

He shook his head. 'Never mind, we'll sort things out. I'm flush, I just finished a job lumping wheat.'

For the next week Chilla worked me like a horse. We ran

a couple of miles each morning and he had me skipping over an old greenhide rope. I sorta got the idea he enjoyed having me there to train with; he knew he'd have to fight Billy Smith some time soon.

Chilla showed me how to shape up and how to move so I wouldn't get caught flat footed. I learned how to slip a left lead and how to counter with a left myself, and he showed me how to throw a straight right – in fact, I became familiar with the full range of punches. Chilla explained that fights were won by smart thinking and guts. A man needed to know how to fight, but it was his head and his heart that made the difference. We did a lot of sparring in the last few days, and he showed me a few things that some English toff he named would not approve of. But he wouldn't come at using the boot. Chilla reckoned anyone who put in the boot deserved all he got.

'Always be on the lookout for king hits, a lot of fights are won that way. If a fella ever gets the better of you, dig him out at daylight next morning. Nine times out of ten you'll beat him.'

At the end of the week, Chilla seemed satisfied that I could hold my own, but insisted that I keep on with the training program he had set me. We hadn't heard from Billy Smith and I was beginning to think that he had dingoed. However, one morning one of his cronies approached our camp, he didn't come too close, mind you. Anyway, from a safe distance, he sang out that Billy Smith was up at the pub and wanted to see Chilla. Chilla says all right he'll be up in half an hour.

'Are you going to fight him?' I asked.

'No, Snowy, not today, and when I do it won't be for nothing. Now, when we go up, I want you to watch my back.'

Well, we walked up to the pub and went into the bar. Smith and three of his mates were talking to the publican. The week's training had given me a lot of confidence, but when we entered that bar, I can tell you, I was packing 'em. Chilla walked straight up to Smith.

'Right,' he said, 'let's fix up this fight for Saturday

afternoon, bare fists, but I don't see why we should knock ourselves around for nothing.' Without pausing, he turned to the publican. 'You can organise it in the pub's back yard, it's secure, charge what you like to get in, you'll sell swags of grog, you'll have to sling the sergeant, but you've probably got him in your pocket already, Billy and I will get two quid each, you fix up for a referee, fighters to get their own seconds, Snowy here will be swinging the towel for me, right then, see you Saturday afternoon.'

With that, he turned on his heel and walked out. I think he said the lot without drawing breath. It was so smooth, it left them staring after him open mouthed. Just the same, as I followed Chilla out I had an overpowering urge to look back. It was the smartest thing I'd ever seen in my life, and I told him so on the way back to the camp.

Chilla stopped and looked at me. 'Snowy, if ever you have to talk your way out of a tight corner, never stop, say what you have to say and get out. If you pause for a second, some smart alec will jump in with a remark and you'll have a blue on your hands. Smith was waiting for me this morning. It was a set up, and as soon as I walked in, I knew.'

For the next two days we worked out and sparred a lot. On Friday night we were sitting around the fire, and I looked over at Chilla and asked him if he was confident of winning the coming fight. He didn't answer for a bit, then with a funny look he said, 'No, Snow, I think Smith will win the fight tomorrow.'

I stared at him in amazement. 'You think Smith will win?'

'Yes, mainly because I plan to help him win. I want a return bout out of this and that won't be possible if I give him a hiding. Don't worry, though, I'll give him a good flogging before it's finished. Tomorrow I want you to put five bob on me, no more. We'll clean up on the return bout and make Billy Smith regret he ever tormented that kid.'

On Saturday after breakfast Chilla and I went for a bit of a run, but he did nothing else. We yarned most of the morning, and after lunch Chilla had a sleep. How he could do that with the fight only a few hours away had me beat.

Just before four o'clock Chilla and I strolled up to the pub. We walked through the bar to the backyard, where there was a crowd of nearly a hundred gathered. The publican had marked off a square boxing ring in the dirt. It was lined by blokes sitting down to give others a view. The referee was the sergeant of police, and I could see that Chilla was pleased about that.

There were stools placed in two corners of the ring with buckets beside them. A timekeeper, full of importance, sat beside the ring clutching a fob watch in one hand and a condamine bell in the other.

Billy Smith came into the ring looking like a professional boxer. He had a shiny satin dressing gown on over boxer shorts. He also had proper boxing boots on. Old Chilla just took off his shirt and tucked the bottom of his trousers into his socks. I was surprised by that, I'd never seen him with socks on before.

I took up my position by Chilla's corner, and after the gloves were inspected I gave him a hand to lace them on. Then the referee called the two fighters into the centre of the ring. Smith had taken off his robe and was dancing around. I reckon the whole display was to put the wind up Chilla. The referee gave them the usual spiel – no hitting below the belt, and all that – then they went back to their corners. The ref nodded to the bloke with the condamine bell. He gave it a shake and the fight was on.

Despite the pug's professional clobber, Chilla gave him a boxing lesson for most of the first round. Then towards the end Chilla kept going into clinches. To most, it would have seemed that Chilla was getting the worst of the close in fighting, but I had learned enough to know that he was taking most of the punishment on his arms and gloves.

At the end of the round, Chilla gave the appearance of being hurt. I could see the pug being urged on by his mates over in the other corner.

'How's it going?' I asked Chilla.

'She's jake, swing that towel around and throw some water over me.'

I managed to get the five bob on Chilla during the second round. Smith had come out strong, but the round was much the same as the first. Towards the bell, Chilla seemed to be getting the worst of things, and the noise from the pug's corner grew. Chilla was back-pedalling and then hanging on. He came back to his corner at the end of the round bent over and gasping for air. He made it look good – in fact, he had me fooled for a bit, but he tipped me the wink, had a mouthful of water and spat it out.

'Get busy with that towel,' he muttered, 'and look worried.'

Over in Smith's corner, his mates were laughing and patting him on the back. As the condamine bell signalled the start of the third round, Chilla got up slowly. Smith rushed him before he got halfway across the ring and ran into a straight left that steadied him up a bit. I smiled to myself – if Chilla was going to lose, he was making it look good. He kept out of trouble for a while, then let Smith catch him in a neutral corner. It was hard to see what was going on, but it ended up with Chilla on the ground.

He was up on his feet at the count of six and back-pedalled to keep out of trouble. In the end, Chilla got caught on the ropes again, there was a flurry of punches and Chilla went down once more. It was obviously all over. When the count got to eight, I threw in the towel for good measure.

As Smith raised both hands above his head, the pug's cronies were dancing round like chooks with their heads cut off. He donned his fancy dressing gown again and came over and shook hands with Chilla, who was still sitting on his stool.

'Good fight, Bill,' Chilla said. 'What about a return bout next Saturday, if I'm up to it?'

'You're on,' said Smith, 'but what about winner takes all, eh?'

Chilla told me later, he nearly fell off the stool when Smith said that. On the way back to camp I noticed a bit of a mouse forming under Chilla's left eye.

'He landed a few on you, eh?'

'Well, I had to let him get a couple home to make it look fair dinkum. He's going to get a bloody surprise next Saturday, though.'

Snow yawned and sat up on the edge of his bed. He rolled a smoke with great deliberation. 'I think we'd better call it a night. You've got to do your cliff hanging act again tomorrow.' I nodded, and fell asleep almost immediately.

I left Snowy still snoring next morning and made an early start on the main roof. I felt a little guilty that we had milked the job to the extent we had, then I ran into trouble with the ridge capping on one of the small gabled roofs – it was in a bad way. I went to breakfast to ask the advice of the main contractor. I found him demolishing a plate of bacon and eggs. He saluted me with a fork, and as soon as his mouth was empty, he inquired as to my progress. When told of the difficulties I was having, he grinned broadly.

'Just the ticket, Simmo, you're sure to get another day out of it now.'

'I'm not worried about that, I want your expert advice on how to fix the bloody thing. It's sprung right away from the roof, and it's impossible for me to hold the blasted ridge cap in place and nail it at the same time.'

'No doubt, you expect a cripple to risk his neck to get you out of trouble.' He grinned. 'All right, all right, I'll come up after breakfast and give you a hand.'

Snowy had just stepped onto the ladder behind me, when the publican came around the corner.

'You're not going up on the roof with that ankle, are you?' he asked. 'You've got to start in the kitchen tomorrow, remember.'

Snowy told him he was merely going up to inspect my work and would be very careful not to further injure his ankle. His progress up the ladder was painful to watch; however, as soon as the publican disappeared, he regained his usual agility. With both of us on the job, the ridge capping was duly nailed in place, and Snowy made his way back to solid ground, after urging me to take my time. With no sign of any clouds, the roof was again getting damned hot, but I decided against using the hall runners. With the steep pitch in the roof, I reckoned I would end up on a magic carpet with a perpendicular flight path.

All in all, I had a bad morning. The heat became oppressive, and the angle of the roof made it difficult to work on. I had barked my knuckles and cut my knee on a protruding piece of iron, so, hot and thirsty, I decided to knock off a little before lunchtime. I still had a fair area of roof to finish, but I thought, to hell with it, and made my way across the roof to where I had left the ladder.

# 6

I stepped off the ladder and straightened up, something that was almost impossible to do on the steeply raked roof. I was hot, thirsty and a bit browned off. I headed for the bar, to be met near the back door by the publican. He looked at me and said, 'Are you twenty-one?'

'Who the hell wants to know?'

He looked confused, and stammered, 'It's just that there's a madman in the bar who's demanding to see Twenty-One. He said he saw him on the roof.'

'Oh, I see. Well, he's probably an old mate of mine. Thanks.'

I went into the bar, with no idea who the so-called madman was, then I spotted him.

'Tommy! Where the hell did you spring from?'

'Twenty-One, you old bastard, I reckoned it was you when I saw you clingin' to that roof like a goanna on a bloody gum tree. Good to see ya again, eh, whadaya reckon, eh?'

He gave me a dig in the ribs with an elbow that almost winded me. 'Whataya goin' to have, get a rum inta ya, eh, whada you reckon?'

I had a rum, and Tommy told me he'd just finished a droving trip with a character called Crying Billy.

'Ya know, that clown was as useful as tits on a boar pig. They weren't bad bullocks, but he couldn't handle 'em. They jumped a bit, and they rushed one night when the watches were changing. Both night horses were out, so I got to the fire where Crying Billy was. You could hear the mob goin' hell for leather through the scrub. He was singing out, "Woah bullocks, woah boys". He turned to me and says, "They know my voice, you know".

' "Well," I said, "they may know your bloody voice, but the bastards would need microphones up their backsides to hear ya." '

Tommy laughed uproariously at his own story. 'Jesus, I'm pleased to see ya, we had some good times together, eh. Remember the time when you got on the rum and threw your crutches away, then climbed up on that pub roof and fought three rounds with the kitchen chimney? Do you remember that, eh, good times, whadaya reckon, eh?'

Before I could answer, he elbowed me in the ribs again. 'Listen, Tommy,' I croaked, 'if you hit me in the ribs again, I'll kick you in the cods.'

Tommy roared with laughter and slapped me on the back. 'The same old Twenty-One,' he roared. 'Jesus, it's good to see you, whada yer reckon, eh?'

Joan, the barmaid, had retreated to the other end of the bar. The publican, seeing that our glasses were empty again, approached hesitantly. No doubt he could see the cost of his roof repairs escalating alarmingly. I put his mind at rest by asking for an advance of a quid on the job. We had another rum, and relived the old days with a great deal of gusto, but I kept a close eye on Tommy's elbow.

I turned around to see Snowy standing behind me. He had obviously been an interested onlooker for some time. I introduced the pair.

'Any mate of Twenty-One's a mate of mine, eh, whadaya reckon?'

Snowy said he reckoned so, and took the rum Tommy handed him.

'You wouldn't believe the things this old bastard and me have been through together,' Tommy said, jerking his thumb in my direction.

Snowy said he didn't doubt it, and added that he had wondered why I had seemed so much at home on the roof.

'Jesus, mate, now I've run into ya, I'd like to stay for a bit, but I'm just passin' through. The bloke I'm with don't drink, the bastard's only stayin' an hour. Another three rums here, boss,' he roared, addressing the publican.

Snowy, who had been regarding Tommy with great interest, suddenly said, 'There's a bloke trying to catch your attention at the door, Tommy.'

'Christ! I've gotta go, fellas. Good to see ya again, Twenty-One, whadaya reckon, eh?' And he was gone.

As I stared out of the door after him, Snowy tapped me on the shoulder.

'The lunch bell has gone, are you going to have a feed, eh, whada ya reckon, eh?'

I told him to get nicked and followed him into the dining room.

We trooped in to find Maisie with a troubled look on her face. 'There's only cold meat and tinned vegetables for lunch – the cook had a few drinks to celebrate her departure.'

'Well,' said Snow, 'we'll all have a drink later to celebrate that.'

'By the smell of you both, I think you've done that already.'

Snowy swallowed a mouthful of dry corned beef. 'That mate of yours, Tommy, he's a bit of a character, isn't he?'

I had to agree. 'Tommy is a bit overpowering when you first meet him, but he's a genuine bloke, and a good mate in a pinch.'

As Maisie removed our plates, Snowy eyed me over his teacup. 'That yarn about you and the pub chimney . . .'

He was interrupted by the entrance of a very drunk ringer who demanded a meal. Maisie told him the dining room was closed, but he persisted. 'Come on, sweetie, I only want a feed.'

I could see Maisie was becoming flustered. Snowy very deliberately got up and walked over to her. The ringer looked him over, decided it would be better to seek nourishment in the bar and departed. Maisie thanked him gratefully, and Snowy, playing the reluctant hero to the full, replied, 'Oh! It was nothing, we can't have drunks in our dining room, can we?'

I finished my tea and stood up. 'Well, I'm off to have a spine bash.'

Snowy caught up with me on the back verandah.

Thankfully he didn't ask me again about the pub chimney.

I stretched out on my swag. 'Well, Snow,' I said, 'I'm pleased you've got the cooking job, but after I finish the roof, I'll have to see about getting something myself.'

'You reckon you might hit the frog and toad?'

'I'll give it a day or two first,' I told him. 'I'm going to miss being entertained by those yarns of yours.'

'Well, I'd better finish the yarn about Chilla's fights with Billy Smith.'

I agreed that was a great idea, and Snowy took up the story with his usual enthusiasm.

Now, where the hell was I up to. Yeah, I remember, we were going back to the camp. Anyway, we hadn't long been there, when the sergeant drove up in a car. He got out and came over with a brown paper bag in his hand. He sat down on a log that doubled for a chair and looked at Chilla.

'What the hell are you up to, O'Rourke? I'm not a fool, you could have taken Smith any time you liked.'

'What's the problem?'

'He's a standover merchant, a hiding would do him a lot of good.'

'Well,' Chilla told him. 'I needed to get a quid out of the business, that's all. Next Saturday, Smith is going to get the father of a hiding.'

'Right,' says the sergeant. 'We'll have a drink on that.'

And he pulls two bottles of beer out of the bag and gives one to Chilla. 'Don't expect any help from me in the ring, you're on your own there.'

Chilla grinned at him. 'All you'll have to do is count him out, but don't be in too much of a hurry.'

After we had a feed that night, Chilla and I talked for a long time. We often did that, it was mainly Chilla giving me the drum about life in general. Apart from telling Chilla about some of my later work experiences, I'd never said anything to him about my younger days. Of course, he'd given me a great lecture on not accepting work for less money than I should have. Anyway, this night as we sat around the fire, I sorta opened up and gave him the full story. When I had finished, Chilla looked at me.

'Well, I've got to admit, Snowy, you're a survivor. I reckon you're a living example of man's instinct of self preservation.'

'What's the strength of this instinct business?' I asked him.

'Well, self preservation is one of the two oldest and most important human drives. The other is the preservation of the tribe or species. Those drives were crucial in the development of primitive man. Together they have taken mankind from caves to cathedrals.'

He could get wound up at times, old Chilla could, but I sorta got the drift of what he was saying, so I asked him about the second one he had mentioned.

'Well,' he said, 'by helping each other, it guaranteed the survival of the group.'

I thought about that for a while, then I said, 'So, to survive, everyone had to get stuck in. What about in war? Did you volunteer because of the survival of the species?'

It was a bit cheeky of me, I suppose, and he gave me a hard look.

'Well, Snow, to be honest, the war was a long way from Australia. In the early days, I think most of us went because of the adventure. But when the casualty lists came out from the Somme in sixteen, there had to be something more than the desire to see the world.'

Chilla didn't like to talk about the war, and I knew I was treading on dangerous ground, but for some reason I felt I had to know more.

'What about this preservation business, then?' I asks him.

He thought for a while, then he looked at me and says, 'It's impossible to describe what went on at the front. You tried to survive, but there were men who risked their lives, and often died, to get their mates out of trouble.'

I thought about that for a minute, then said, 'Chilla, do you think my old man might have been killed like that?'

He sorta gives me a funny look, then he says. 'Yes, Snow,

I suppose that is possible, he may well have been killed like that.'

That night, before I went to sleep, I thought a bit about my old man. Well, as I'd never met him, I couldn't really think about him, I suppose, I just imagined what he might have been like.

Anyway, bugger me if I didn't dream about him that night, and it was the craziest bloody dream I ever had. I met my old man in France, and that was impossible because I was a baby when he was killed. Anyway, as I said, I met him, but he was fighting with the Germans.

I looked at my mate. 'How the blazes did you work that out?'

'Well, he had this German helmet on, and he was sitting on the edge of this shell hole eating a big German sausage.'

I couldn't help myself, I laughed. 'You're pulling my leg.'

'No, mate, this is dinkum. He saw me walking up, and he waved the sausage and said, "Hello, son, how's your mother's chooks?"

' "Stuff the chooks," I told him. "Why are you fighting with the Germans?"

' "Oh, it doesn't matter who we fight for, we're all going to be killed anyway, but the tucker's better over here." And he took a bite of the bloody great sausage.'

'Well, what happened then?' I asked Snow.

'There must have been more, but I don't remember anything else. Flamin crazy, eh?'

I had to agree with my mate, but assured him that dreams often were pretty weird. Snowy was silent for a little while, then took up the story again.

Anyway, Chilla took things pretty easy after the fight. We had a run in the morning, then a bit of a spar in the evenings. I thought he might have been taking Smith too lightly, but he laughed.

'Don't worry, Snowy. Having fought Smith, I know how good he is. I don't have to knock myself about to be ready for him.'

So we took things easy and he continued with my education, as he called it. Edgar, the grey-haired bloke I saw the first day, sometimes came over to our camp at night and yarned with Chilla. He was a pommy and, according to Chilla, he was an Oxford man, whatever that was. The grog had apparently done him out of a professional career. He always called everyone by their surname, and I reckoned he was a bit of a red rag'er. I asked Chilla if he was a commo. There was a lot of talk about commos then.

'No,' Chilla said, 'I'd call him a free thinker.'

Anyway, this night they got stuck into politics. Chilla was disgusted with the Labor Government over the way they'd deserted the striking coal miners.

'You've got to remember, O'Rourke,' Edgar says, 'that Scullin is not a strong man, he knows as much about economics as my backside knows about snipe shooting. The man is putty in the hands of the bankers.'

'But surely Theodore should be able to stand up for Labor policy – after all, he is treasurer.'

'Perhaps, but it was Theodore who gave that guarantee to the coal miners. You've got to realise there are powerful forces moving against the Scullin government. Look what's happening in this state – the banks are calling the tune, and Bavin is dancing to it. He believes that the only way to get the economy back on its feet is to cut wages and costs.'

Chilla chipped in. 'This state is becoming the worst hit by the depression, and if you limit the spending power of the people, things can only get worse. And the fear and uncertainty he's causing among workers is likely to encourage scabbing.'

'Well, O'Rourke, that won't bother the man, it will do the job for him.'

I had been listening to all this and decided to put my spoke in. 'Hang on,' I said, 'how can you blame a bloke with a wife and a couple of kids for taking what's offering?'

'That is a reasonable question, young man,' said Edgar. He was a patronising bastard. 'The trouble is that once men start to compete for jobs by accepting less money and poorer conditions, everyone becomes worse off.'

But I wasn't finished yet. 'Well, the employers must be better off, and they should be able to employ more men.'

Chilla gave me one of his looks and decided to take over my education. 'Well, Snowy, they are better off for a short period, but you've got to remember, if people get less money, they spend less. Soon producers, manufacturers, shopkeepers and tradesmen feel the pinch. It becomes a vicious circle, a poverty-stricken merry-go-round that everyone would like to get off, but can't.'

That sorta put me in my place, so I left them to it and crawled into me swag.

'Well, mate, if I'm going to finish that roof tomorrow morning, I'd better crawl out of the swag and do some work. You can tell me the rest of the yarn tonight.'

Fortunately I was working on the shaded side of the roof and the job went along smoothly during the afternoon. By knock off time I estimated I could finish it in a couple of hours the next morning. I imagined the publican would heave a huge sigh of relief to be at last rid of his freeloading roof repairer.

I had a clean up and went into the bar, where Snowy was chatting to the barmaid. After a couple of drinks, we adjourned to the dining room, and walked into the middle of a culinary crisis. Maisie was in tears. She told us that the cook had got stuck into the grog and had fallen asleep, slumped over the kitchen table. She and the missus had done what they could to salvage the dinner, but all they had to offer was a badly burnt stew and soggy vegetables. Both she and the publican's wife were apologetic, but we assured them that we had both eaten worse. And that was no lie.

I looked at Snow. 'I reckon the old girl has done you a favour. Anything you dish up has to be an improvement on this.'

Snow nodded. Just then a disturbance from the kitchen

indicated that the cook had surfaced and was raising merry hell. Maisie, white faced, came and sat at our table.

'I'm not going back in there, I don't care if the washing up doesn't get done tonight.'

'Don't worry about it,' Snowy told her. 'We'll sort things out in the morning. Chilla always said that you can neither reason with drunken women nor flatten 'em.'

We finished dinner, with the cook still treating the pots and pans to a tirade of drunken abuse. I left Snowy talking to Maisie and went for a walk.

Snowy was still missing when I got back. As it turned out, he had stayed to give Maisie a hand after the publican had frog-marched the cook to her room. I didn't hear him come to bed, but next morning he woke me up as he rummaged around trying to find his boots. It was not yet daylight, the roof was under control, so I decided to enjoy a lie in. I went back to sleep wondering what my mate would serve up as his first meal.

The breakfast bell woke me and, feeling a bit guilty, I had a clean up and hastened to the dining room to see what was on offer. Everything seemed to be back to normal. Maisie arrived from the kitchen and placed a plate of corned beef fritters in front of me, supplemented by a dollop of bubble and squeak.

'What, no steak and eggs?' I asked her.

'No, Snowy said to tell everyone that there's practically nothing left in the pantry or the fridge. He said he'd have to order a stack of groceries and meat later in the morning.'

I laughed. 'The revenge of the spurned cook, Maisie. That will teach him not to give her cheek from the kitchen roof.'

I thoroughly enjoyed the breakfast, I've always been partial to Burdekin ducks, the bushman's name for fritters. I thought that Snow had done rather well with what he had to work with. After a leisurely second cup of tea and a smoke, I wandered out and stood looking up at the small area of roof I had to finish. The publican joined me. 'Do you think you'll finish today?' he asked hopefully.

I told him a couple of hours would see the job finished. He didn't actually heave a sigh of relief, but it must have been touch and go.

I hauled the ladder over to the edge of the roof and, collecting hammer and nails, climbed up to the job for the last time. Half an hour before lunch I drove the final nail home. The job was finished, but it had been a beauty while it lasted – Snowy's contract price arrangement had been a stroke of genius. I climbed down the ladder for the last time and put it and the hammer away. I then walked into the bar to find the publican.

He saw me and came over. 'All finished?'

I nodded and he went over to the till and returned with nine quid and handed it to me.

'Your mate said to give you the full amount, as he was doing the cooking now.'

I thanked him, ordered a beer and invited him to join me. We talked for a while about things in general and cooks in particular. He seemed very grateful to Snowy for stepping into the breach. We agreed he was a fine chap, then, as the lunch bell rang, I excused myself and strolled into the dining room. Maisie came out of the kitchen looking slightly worried. 'Snowy said to apologise again, the stores were delivered late. There's only fritters and salad for lunch.'

'That's all right, Maisie,' I said, wondering to myself if Snowy's expertise in the kitchen was limited to cooking Burdekin ducks.

As I was finishing the meal, Snowy came into the dining room, I thanked him for foregoing his part of the roof payment.

'By the way, can you cook anything else beside bloody Burdekin ducks?'

'Oh! Ye of little faith,' he grinned.

'Never mind quoting Chilla to me. I can see myself looking like a Burdekin duck before I leave here.'

'Well, you'll just have to wait and see.' With that, he returned to the kitchen, leaving me still wondering.

I was strolling down the pub verandah after lunch when the publican called me into the bar. 'You're looking for a job, aren't you?'

I assured him I was. 'Well, there's a chap from out of town looking for a man. I told him you'd probably be interested.'

'My bloody oath I'm interested.'

'Well, he's leaving town about four. He'll call here on the way out.'

I thanked him and went to tell Snowy the news. I found him in the kitchen in the middle of unpacking and stowing things away.

'That's great, but it's a pity in one way – you may go to your grave never knowing if I can cook anything besides Burdekin ducks.'

'Well, that's something I'll just have to learn to live with. When you get through what you're doing, come into the bar and we'll have a few drinks together.'

I rolled up my swag and left it on the front verandah. I then went into the bar, ordered a beer and waited for Snowy to join me.

He strolled in a little later, and I ordered another beer.

'Well, Simmo,' he said, raising his glass, 'here's to the future. Do you know how long the job will last?'

I had to admit that I hadn't talked to the chap myself yet, but hoped I would get a few months out of it.

'Well, mate, if I don't see you again, all the best. I've got to go now and start dinner. I'll try and see you off, though.'

A little after four, a battered truck pulled up in front of the pub. I introduced myself and was told to throw my swag on the back. I shook hands with Snowy, who had arrived in time to see me off. I was getting into the front of the truck, when my mate sang out, 'Hey! I didn't tell you who won the return bout.'

'Well, who did?'

The truck started to pull away and Snowy's shouted reply was lost in the roar of the engine.

75

# 7

A month after I'd left Snowy as lord and master of the kitchen, I landed back in town. It was about four o'clock in the afternoon, and, throwing my swag on the hotel verandah, I walked into the bar. Joan, the barmaid, who I recognised from my first visit, gave me a welcoming smile.

'Hello, you're Snowy's mate, aren't you? What would you like?'

I nodded to the first part of her question, and ordered a beer. I had not paid a great deal of attention to the barmaid when last in town, but having money in the pocket makes a hell of a difference to a man's demeanour. When she came back with my drink, I introduced myself properly. The bar was almost deserted, so I took the opportunity to have a yarn. I learnt that Joan was from Brisbane, she liked being up country and enjoyed seeing how the other half lived.

Just then the publican's wife came into the bar and greeted me with, 'Back again! Snowy will be pleased to see you.'

I said hello, then asked, 'He's still here, then?'

'Oh yes, Snowy is still here, but he's not cooking now.'

'I'm not surprised. Tell me, can he cook anything besides fritters?'

She laughed. 'Initially I had doubts myself – after the stores came, I waited to see how he performed. The night you left, he put on a three course dinner, and he was disappointed you weren't here to sample his menu. I was impressed, he is quite a good cook, really. Nothing fancy, mind you, but good solid meals. After ten days or so, I could see he was getting bored. As luck would have it, a chap who used to cook for us at our last hotel turned up, and Snowy was happy to hand over the pots and pans.'

'So, he's a man of leisure?'

'Oh no! Just after the new cook started, our yardman got on the booze. He had been off it for so long, we thought he had it beaten. It was a pity, but we had to let him go. We talked to Snowy and he agreed to help us out again.'

I smiled inwardly, I could see the hand of my mate in the yardman's downfall. Creating a market, Chilla had called it.

'You'll be staying with us for a while?'

'Well, yes, but I don't think I can afford to stay at the pub.'

She thought for a minute. 'There are two bunks in Snowy's room. We're not allowed to put paying guests there, but if Snowy has no objection, you can bunk there.'

I started to thank her, when she interrupted me. 'Speak of the devil,' she said, 'here's the man himself.'

I turned to see Snowy enter the bar. He caught sight of me and, grinning broadly, came over. 'How the hell are you, Simmo?'

I told him I was both fit and financial. 'Right, let's have a beer. We'll shake this old town up a bit now you're back and we've both got a quid.'

We had a few beers and went in to dinner in high spirits. 'By the way,' I said as we sat down, 'the missus said I could doss in your room, if it's all right with you.'

Snowy hesitated a moment, then said, 'That's fine by me, but I may not always be there, if you know what I mean.'

'Look, if it's not convenient, don't worry about it,' I told him, then quickly changed the subject as Maisie appeared.

She seemed delighted to see me; however, I sensed a hint of embarrassment. It was not hard to see that their relationship had blossomed in my absence.

After dinner we had a few more beers, then Snowy showed me to his room. I threw my swag on the spare bed and looked over at my mate.

'The yardman breaking out on the grog must have been handy for you. I don't suppose you had anything to do with it?'

'Well, he may have seen me plant a bottle of rum – his skin was cracking, anyway, and it was only a matter of time before he broke out. I reckoned the timing might as well suit me.'

Snowy told me about Maisie. They were going steady, he said. I hid my surprise – going steady was a complete reversal of my mate's usual methods of dealing with the fair sex. He didn't look particularly happy about the situation. I was intrigued, but had no intention of becoming involved in Snowy's affairs of the heart.

Remembering his hesitation at dinner when I told him about sharing the room, I said, 'Any time you want the room to yourself, just give me the nod.' Then, to change the subject, I said, 'Tell me about the return bout. I couldn't hear a word you said above the noise of the truck.'

Snowy brightened at once...

Oh, Chilla gave him a real flogging. He wouldn't knock Smith out, though, just cut him to pieces. His corner threw in the towel a couple of times, but the old sergeant, who was refereeing the fight again, just kicked it out of the ring. In the end, Smith wouldn't come out of his corner.

The crowd was bigger than at the first fight and keen to bet on Smith, so I had no trouble getting money on Chilla. At first, the noise of the mob was deafening, but it slowly died down, and towards the end, there was a stunned silence as Chilla cut loose. No doubt there was a fair bit of dough lost on Smith, and the crowd gave him hell when he dingoed. After the fight, the coppers escorted him away from the pub for his own safety.

The publican was holding the bets, and when things had quietened down a bit, he called us into the office and settled up. Chilla and I picked up twenty quid, with prize money and wagers. The publican shook hands with Chilla and told him the blokes in the public bar wanted to buy him a drink. They made a big fuss of Chilla in the bar, slapping him on the back and telling him what a great bloke he was. For a long time afterwards Chilla became a sorta hero figure in the town. It seemed everyone was tickled pink to see Smith knocked off his perch. It didn't impress old Chilla much, though. 'Never put your faith in fair-weather friends, Snow,' he told me. 'They'll wipe you like a dirty backside the moment the sun stops shining.'

It was a good camp on the waterhole and, being cashed up, we were in no hurry to leave. Edgar was a fairly regular visitor in the evenings and brought Chilla up to date with his theories on solving the depression. Things seemed to be going from bad to worse. I remember Edgar saying that two hundred men had turned up at the Sydney work exchange when relief work was offered – most went away empty handed. Unemployment was getting worse all over the world, and it seemed to me that no one had any answers. Chilla, though, still reckoned that Theodore – Red Ted, he called him – would sort things out.

A few days after the fight, Chilla got word that the sergeant of police would like to see him. Chilla thought about that for a day or so; he was never in a hurry to accommodate the long arm of the law. Finally, one afternoon, he strolled up to the police station, and insisted that I go along with him, saying, 'When you're dealing with the wallopers, always have a witness.'

The police station was a wooden building next door to the sergeant's house. We found him with his feet on his desk reading a copy of *Smith's Weekly*. We removed our hats and took the seats he indicated. Fat seemed to be an occupational hazard with most police sergeants those days, but this bloke was a big, raw-boned character and one of the fittest-looking coppers I remember meeting.

He folded *Smith's Weekly* carefully, put it down and looked at Chilla.

'Ah, O'Rourke, I see you've brought your second with you. Thanks for coming, anyway.' He brought his boots down to the floor with a thump. 'I've got a proposition to put to you.' He rubbed his chin thoughtfully.

'I wouldn't ask this of a lot of men, but I believe you're a man of some principle, and the kids here seem to worship you.' He stopped as though uncertain as to what to say next. I hadn't a bloody clue what the old bastard was talking about, but Chilla was a wake up.

He looked at the sergeant. 'It's about the kids, then?'

'Yes,' the sergeant said, and you could see he was relieved that Chilla had picked up his drift. 'The kids here are not a bad lot, but most of their parents are on the breadline, and a lot of them are living in shanties, with their fathers away carrying their swags God knows where.'

He stopped for a minute and looked at Chilla to see his reaction.

Chilla gave him a hard look. 'You don't have to spell it out to me, I've carried my swag with the poor bastards and seen them hounded from one police station to the next.'

'Yes, yes. Well, we won't go into that here,' muttered the sergeant. 'I want to do something for the kids, and I'd like your help.'

'Fair enough,' said Chilla. 'What's on your mind?'

'Well, there used to be a police youth club here years ago. It was located in the School of Arts hall. I believe some of the gear is still in a back room there. Most of it will be in bad shape, but, with your help, I'd like to try and get the youth club going again.'

Chilla surprised me by getting up and going over and looking out a window. After a minute or so, he turned around and asked, 'Who were the club's last office bearers, are the club's books still around, and is there any money left in the club's account?'

The sergeant shook his head. 'No, I've looked for the books, and had no luck. The bank said the balance was withdrawn and the account closed by the secretary. I know what you're thinking, O'Rourke, but all this happened before my time here. Crying over spilt milk won't change anything, I'd rather do something for the kids now.'

Chilla sat down again, but seemed far from convinced. The sergeant thumped the desk with his fist.

'Look, O'Rourke, I'm an honest man, and I'll throw this uniform off and go out the back with any man who says I'm not.'

Chilla grinned at him, it was the type of language he understood. 'Fair enough, Tom, I'm with you, but I won't be a party to any club. We do this ourselves or not at all.'

They shook hands, and the sergeant looked at Chilla. 'All right, no club. But what about money for gear?'

'Well, the first thing to do is to see what we've got. If you're free, let's go and check the stuff at the hall.'

'Right you are,' said the copper. 'I found the hall keys the other day. Hop in the car and we'll see what's there.'

We piled into the police vehicle, a Chev Tourer, and the sergeant pulled around at the back of the School of Arts hall. It was badly in need of a coat of paint, but the back door opened easily enough at the turn of the key. The back room was a jumble of broken tables and chairs and other junk, but right at the back of the mess, we found what we were looking for. We dragged the gear from the old youth club into the backyard and looked it over. The parallel bars were in fair shape, as were the two vaulting horses – except for the pads. There were two speed bags – a bit dry, with the bladders perished beyond repair – and a heavy punching bag that the rats had gutted. Rats and mice had also destroyed the two pairs of boxing gloves, but the mittens would do with a bit of leather dressing. The leather thongs of the skipping ropes would have to be replaced, but the stools and water buckets had survived without damage. There was also a portable ring that could do with a few repairs.

The sergeant pushed his hat back and scratched his head. 'Well, O'Rourke, what do you think?'

Chilla pulled the bladder out of the second speed ball and stood up. He put his boot into the heavy bag. 'We'll run the gloves, those bladders and the heavy bag down to the dump. On the way back, we'll call in on the saddler and get him to replace the pads on the horses and fix new thongs to the

*The sergeant pushed his hat back and scratched his head. 'Well, O'Rourke, what do you think?'.*

skipping rope handles. We can also get some leather dressing for the speed balls and the mittens from him. That leaves only gloves and a heavy bag to get.'

Chilla was fired up with enthusiasm now. The sergeant started to say something, but Chilla had the bit between his teeth. 'I've got a few contacts in Sydney. There's bound to be a couple of gyms there feeling the pinch, I'll ring around. We should be able to come up with some used gear pretty cheap.' He paused, and reaching into his hip pocket, he pulled out a fiver.

'Here, cover that, Tom, and we'll hit the publican for a brick. With a bit of help from the other shops, we'll have this show on the road.'

The sergeant pushed his hat back and chuckled. He handed a fiver to Chilla. 'Here, you look after the funds.'

The saddler was a grizzled old character who was reputed to have been a top horseman in his day. Chilla put him in the picture and asked for his help. We walked out with two free tins of leather dressing and a fifty per cent discount on the work needed.

The sergeant dropped us off at the pub and returned to the station. He was a rare bird, all right. During the depression, the milk of human kindness, as they call it, did not run too strongly in the veins of most wallopers.

Chilla put the fangs into the publican. He looked doubtful, then finally spoke. 'The last youth club here folded when the sergeant left, taking the funds with him. I won't be involved in another club.'

Chilla assured him there was no club, just a few people trying to help the kids. 'Look, I made money out of those fights I had, and so did you. I just want to help the town by giving a bit back. You've got my word, it's no con job.'

After a moment's thought, the publican went to the till and extracted a tenner. 'Right, Chilla, there you are, but no more, that's it.'

Chilla thanked him. 'Just a couple of things. Do you have two old mattresses we can borrow, and can I use your phone to ring Sydney about getting some gear up?'

'Jesus Christ! How are you off for socks and underpants?'

Chilla grinned. 'I never wear 'em, thanks all the same. Now, where's the phone?'

We carried the speed bags and the boxing mittens back to camp to soften them up with leather dressing. On the way, I decided to have a shot at Chilla for being so matey with a walloper. He propped and eyed me sternly.

'Look, Snow, even if we're dealing with coppers, this idea of helping the kids is top drawer. The end will justify the means. Remember good can sometimes come out of bad – the best mushrooms grow in dung. In this life, there will be times when you'll have to dance with the Devil. If you do, make sure people know that you're calling the tune.'

Old Chilla never missed a chance to further my education. I used to think he was a bloody oracle, and I reckon he was smart in a lot of ways. Looking back, though, I think a lot of his wisdom was borrowed – not that there's anything wrong with that, I suppose, is there?

I assured Snowy that nobody is born wise, and that original thought is a very scarce commodity.

He finished rolling a smoke and looked relieved. 'That's what I reckoned.'

Anyway, back at the camp we slapped leather dressing on the gear, then got stuck into a good-sized rabbit that had been roasting in a homemade camp oven. It went pretty well with a bit of bread and fat, all washed down with sweet black billy tea. My luck certainly changed for the better after meeting up with Chilla. Before that, I had seen a lot more dinnertimes than dinners. Any man who went to his swag those days with a full stomach was a bloody lucky man. The depression was ruining the lives of God knows how many people, and work was becoming nonexistent, but there I was with a good meal under my belt, yarning around the fire without a care in the world.

Edgar came over later, brimming with news. Bavin, he claimed, had finally overstepped the mark. In cutting the wages of the public servants, he had soiled his own nest. Labor was assured of victory at the next state election. The 'Big Fella', Jack Lang, would then soon sort things out.

He wasn't so chirpy about the Federal Government, though. It continued to be a big disappointment to him and Chilla. Theodore was under investigation for some mining scandal up here in Queensland and Scullin was dithering around, 'like a gin at a christening,' he said. I left them talking about the failure of unions in times of crisis, and crawled into the swag.

In the next three days Chilla and I cleaned the hall out, and repaired the ring and set it up. Next day there was a message at the pub for Chilla – the gear he had ordered from Sydney would be on Saturday's train.

When the day arrived, Chilla got the sergeant to drive us to the station. After picking up the boxing equipment, we went to the saddlers, then to the pub for the mattresses. That afternoon we set everything up, and stood back to admire our handiwork. 'Right,' said Chilla, 'all we need now are the kids.'

The sergeant walked over to the heavy bag and drove a solid right cross into it. He looked at Chilla. 'What times are you going to operate?'

Chilla gave that some thought. 'I think we'll open for an hour in the evenings, three times a week, and on Saturday mornings.'

'Right, on Monday I'll go around the schools and let them know the set up.'

There were two primary schools in the town, a state school and a small convert school run by the nuns. In the evening sessions on the first week, six or seven kids turned up. They were well dressed and well behaved, but Chilla wasn't happy. 'These kids are from good homes, and their parents are not short of money. They're not the lads that need our help. Tomorrow afternoon we're going to do some door knocking.'

Door knocking is what we did, although a lot of the houses didn't have doors. We started in a poor area down near the railway. You know, Simmo, I reckon you can smell poverty. Not that the places were dirty, they weren't, but that was the impression I went away with. Because of Chilla's reputation, we got a good hearing. When it was made plain there was no cost, we got plenty of support. At one house, the boy who had been Smith's victim answered our call. He ran back inside, yelling to his father that Mr O'Rourke was at the door.

I've seen some broken men in my time, but that bloke took the belt. Life had apparently kicked him in the guts until he had thrown in the towel. The shame of his being unable to cope was written all over him. We talked for a while and enrolled the lad.

We finished up at some shanties on the edge of town. They mostly housed families whose breadwinner was away carrying their swag somewhere. The shanties were constructed of bags, flattened kerosene tins and anything else that would help to keep the weather out. I think that they must have been erected on the town common, for there were no streets or roads, and the only water was from a council bore a couple of hundred yards away. You know, you read a lot about the hardships suffered by men during the depression, but it was the womenfolk I always felt sorry for. There they were, these mothers, battling to raise families, and trying to retain some respectability in abject poverty – they didn't even own the shanties they were living in. I still get a sick feeling in my guts when I think about those women. I went away with a feeling of shame, and Chilla didn't speak for a long time afterwards. But we picked up ten starters from the shanty area.

From that point on, the attendance was always over thirty. The kids from the poorer parts of town stood out because of their clothes, but Chilla came down hard on any class distinction. The first time the sergeant saw the full group, he did a double take.

'Well, you've got a motley lot here, O'Rourke.'

Chilla gave him that hard look of his. 'We've got to concentrate on the kids who need help the most. They've got no future unless someone can give them some self respect and hope.'

Chilla continued training the kids for six weeks, then he began putting on boxing tournaments on Saturday nights – usually ten bouts of three rounds. There was no nomination fee, and no entry charge, so the town people rolled up for some free entertainment. Each winner received a five bob prize. I know this came out of Chilla's pocket, as the money raised initially had long gone.

At the end of three months, the gym had been accepted by the whole town, and Chilla was even more popular than he'd been after his fight with Smith. Chilla didn't only teach self defence; he talked to the kids about life and how to cope with the problems they would face. It brought about a remarkable change in the lads from the poor areas; they were brimming with confidence, and you could see that they regarded the world as a less hostile place.

Despite the success of the venture, I felt that Chilla was becoming bored. I wondered how long it would be before he decided to move on. In the end, the decision was made for him. One Friday morning the sergeant drove up to the camp. He walked over with a face like thunder. Chilla got up.

'What's up, Tom?'

'I've been transferred at short notice, with a strong reprimand.'

We gaped at him. 'What the hell for?'

Tom sat down on his heels. 'The bastards say I've been getting too familiar with the less desirable elements of the town. I'm afraid it's the end of the gym. They're sending Bluey Porter out to take over.'

Chilla swore. 'Can they do that? What about an appeal?'

Tom shook his head. 'No chance. But it's been good knowing you, O'Rourke. I've got no regrets, but I am bloody annoyed.'

'Well, Tom, same here, but I'll see this Porter about keeping the gym going.'

The sergeant stood up. 'Well, good luck, but I don't like your chances. Porter is a hard man, and he will have his instructions.' He shook hands with us and departed.

Chilla kept the gym going, and two days later he and I went up to the police station to meet the new sergeant. An overweight, red-headed character was sitting at the desk. He looked up.

'What the hell do you want?'

Chilla walked right up to the desk. 'I'm here to see you about keeping the kids' gym going.'

'Oh, are you, and who the hell are you?'

'My name's O'Rourke.'

'Well, Mr O'Rourke, the club is finished. By twelve o'clock today, I want the books together, with details of the club's bank account on this desk.'

Chilla put both hands on the desk and laughed in his face. 'Bad luck, sergeant, there's no club, and no bank account. You'll have to find another source of revenue.'

The sergeant stood up. He wasn't a pretty picture – his face was as red as a beetroot, and a huge gut hung over his belt. 'Get out of here before I charge you with vagrancy,' he snarled. We left, with Chilla giving him a mock salute at the door.

That night we gave the sad news to the kids. You could see they were disappointed, but they took it well enough. Chilla told them how proud he was of them, and they went away with their heads held high. Chilla had made a hell of a difference to their lives. As you know, Simmo, I had a tough time as a kid, and I felt bloody good about being a party to helping those poor little beggars.

Snowy yawned. 'Well, mate, unlike you, I've got to be up at sparrow's chirp to start on the yard. I'll see you in the morning.'

# 8

I woke up before daylight next morning. In the bush, work always starts as soon as it is light enough to see, and old habits die hard. That particular morning, however, I decided to take advantage of the chance to lie in. I heard Snowy get up and depart, remarking that it would take a surgical operation to remove the blankets from some people.

Although I was paying for my meals, the publican's wife told me I could eat in the kitchen. At breakfast that morning, there were four of the staff at the large table – Snowy, Maisie, the laundress and the cook. The babbler was one of those rare characters who combined culinary skills with a happy nature. It was the laundress, a woman of part Aboriginal blood, who interested me most, though. I had a yarn to her later, in the laundry. She told me she had married a white drover and had cooked for his men on the road for a number of years.

'When the kids were old enough to go to school,' she said, 'I told the old bastard 'e would 'ave to pay for a cook, and brought the kids into town. I want my kids to 'ave a decent heducation.'

She was a remarkable woman who had overcome her misfortunes and was determined to give her children a chance in life. I hoped the kids she was battling to educate never showed embarrassment at the way their mother spoke.

Later in the morning I had a stroll around the town and called in at the saddler's shop. There were three ringers sitting around yarning with the saddler as he counterlined a saddle. It's a strange thing, but bushmen are drawn to a saddler's shop like blowflies to a damp blanket. The man plying the seating awl was typical of bush saddlers; he could tell a good yarn without missing a stitch, and obviously did not mind the company. No doubt, he knew they would probably buy something before they left the shop.

Being at a loose end in a small town did not hold a great attraction for me. I had done a bit of saddling on stations where I'd worked, and after the others left, I asked the saddler if he needed a hand. He looked over his glasses at me, then after a minute or so, he asked if I knew anything about packs.

I told him that I'd done up a few. After another pause, he put down the awl, took off his glasses and, turning on his stool, looked directly at me. 'You have, eh. Well, in a day or so I'm expecting a swag of packsaddles from two stations. They'll want 'em back as soon as possible in case the season breaks. If you like, you can strip them down and sew on the new collar check; I'll tack it on for you, though.'

I told him that would suit me down to the ground, and returned to the pub for lunch. Snowy grinned when I told him and, looking at me over a fork loaded with corned beef, remarked, 'Once again, you've proved that the old saying is true.'

'What old saying?' asked Maisie.

'That it's better to be born lucky than born good looking.'

Bush repartee is heavily loaded with tongue-in-cheek insults. Maisie, not understanding, looked shocked. Snowy reassured her. 'Don't worry, what would embarrass Simmo would kill a flamin' horse.'

I didn't see Snowy after lunch, and as we lay on our bunks that night he seemed rather subdued. I thought he must have had a tiff with Maisie. I had come to look forward to his yarns, and he seldom needed prompting to regale me with the exploits of his mate Chilla. But that night was different. Looking over, I had a go at prompting him.

'The depression must have ruined a lot of lives?'

'Yeah, you can say that all right, but there were some

good times. Did I ever tell you about the time I lost my virginity?'

I laughed. 'No, Snow.'

He brightened up a bit. 'It was Chilla's doing, of course. I'll tell you about it one day.'

He lapsed back into gloomy silence.

I decided to give it one more shot.

'Did you stay long in that town, Snow?'

'What town was that?' he asked absently.

'The bloody town where you ran the boxing club,' I said, exasperated.

'Oh, that town? No, we didn't hang about there long. Chilla reckoned that we were better to move fast, seeing that the sergeant was such a bastard.

'Things had got a lot worse. There was a fair bit of unrest about and the wallopers had begun arresting blokes they regarded as troublemakers. There was plenty to complain about, mind you. People were being evicted from rented premises, and mortgagees were selling up private homes and farms left right and centre.'

Snowy was away. He rolled a smoke, lit it, and continued. 'To make matters worse, winter had set in and looked like being as cold as Bavin's charity. There was a cold wind blowing up the kilts of the politicians, too. Labor was sure to win the next New South Wales election. According to Chilla and Edgar, the "Big Fella", Jack Lang, would put things right. In Canberra, though, Labor was in trouble. To Chilla's disgust, Theodore had been forced to resign due to the inquiry into that mining scandal.'

'What about Scullin?' I asked.

Snowy shook his head. 'He was out of his depth, according to Chilla, and had asked a bloke from the Bank of England to come and help us out. When he heard the news, Chilla shook his head. "How the hell is he going to cure our unemployment? They've got over two million of their bloody own."

'Edgar snorted. "He's not here to cure anything, just to make sure we keep paying our debts to England."

'Things were in a bloody mess, I can tell you. The only good news was sporting news – Australia had won the ashes, Bradman belting 334 off the Pom bowlers in the Leeds test.'

I looked at Snowy. 'How the blazes do you remember all this?'

'Mate, you couldn't forget a bloody day of it, even if you wanted to, and l have done a bit of research since. Anyway, to get back to the yarn ...

Edgar had decided to move on, too, but being a man of some means, he intended to pay his train fare out of the joint. Chilla persuaded him to help us depart by train as well – but without the benefit of tickets. The shearing industry was in turmoil, but wool trains were passing through the town every day or so. It was cold, showery weather and Chilla said that the wool would be covered by tarps, as wet wool could burst into flames from some kind of combustion, I forget the term he used.

Anyway, he said it was an ideal set up for train jumping. The plan was for Edgar to go up to the railway station and buy a ticket on the next mixed goods train to pass through the town at night. He then came back and told Chilla he was booked to leave at seven-thirty p.m. the next night.

We had got a fair bit of camp gear together while at the waterhole. It had been a good camp and I was sorry to leave it. Next morning Chilla told me to lighten my swag and throw away anything that wasn't essential.

'You travel light when you're train jumping,' he said, tossing away the homemade camp oven. We ended up with thin swags, one set of tuckerbags, a waterbag and two billies between us. By seven o'clock that night it was dark, and the three of us walked towards the town. Halfway up, we stopped and shook hands with Edgar. Chilla and I then circled around and finished up where Chilla reckoned the wool trucks would stop. A few minutes later we heard the train approaching. It finally ground to a stop with the wool wagons right in front of us. We walked along and when

Chilla found a half-full wagon, he untied a couple of the tarp ropes and threw the cover back. I was about to climb into the wagon, when I felt Chilla's hand on my shoulder.

'Never ever get onto a train with your swag on your back.'

He didn't say anything else, just threw his swag and gear on and followed it. I would soon get to see that it was bloody good advice.

Chilla let the tarp drop back into place, hooking the ropes up as though they were still tied. It was a grouse possie, as warm and dry as you could wish. We settled back on the wool bales, and within a few minutes I went off to sleep, thinking that jumping the rattler was as easy as falling off a log.

I was disturbed later that night by a lot of banging and jarring as the goods train shunted. Chilla was awake and seemed to be expecting something. As the train finally pulled out, the tarp was thrown back, two hands grasped the side of the wagon and a head appeared. The man had a large, untidy swag on his back and struggled to get in. In a flash Chilla grabbed him by the arms and heaved him into the wagon. He sat down, clanking like a tinker's cart. He was a soft-looking bloke in his early twenties, and was obviously out of condition. He sat breathing heavily, then after a minute he looked up and thanked Chilla.

Chilla gave him one of his hard looks.

'I don't know how many trains you've caught, but if you keep that up, you won't be jumping many more.'

As he was speaking, the pylons of a small bridge slid past perilously close to the side of the rail wagon. Chilla jerked his thumb at it and said, 'There's one bloody good reason why you always throw your swag on first. Sure, you could lose your swag if you miss getting on, but that's better than losing your life.'

The young train jumper's face was as white as chalk. 'No one ever told me that,' he said in a shocked voice. 'I've heard lots of fellows talk about train jumping, and they all said it was easy.'

'Most things are easy, if you know what you're doing,' Chilla said. 'But you have to be bloody careful if you're train jumping. Blokes have been killed trying to jump the rattler.'

The train jumper looked at Chilla with awe. 'I'll bet you've jumped a few trains. Have you ever ridden the buffers?'

'I have once, but only because I had no other option. Take my advice and never try it. If you doze off, you won't wake up in this world.'

I looked at Chilla in amazement. 'You mean you sat on those things that keep the rail wagons apart. Didn't anyone see you?'

'Yes, the train crew knew I was there. But most of them are all right.'

It had started to drizzle again, so Chilla put the tarp back in place and we settled down to catch some sleep. I woke up again later and asked Chilla what the time was – old Chilla always carried a gun metal pocket watch.

'It's half past three, and we're at Bogan Gate. I'm pretty sure the train stops to take on water between here and Parkes. We'll leave it then and walk in to the town.'

Sure enough, half an hour later the goods train stopped. Chilla drew the tarp back and peered out.

'Right, the coast's clear, throw your swag out and let's get out to the road.'

As soon as we gathered our swags and gear, we struck out for the main road. I had heard the other bloke stirring as I left the wool wagon but had no idea if he had followed us – you don't hang around after jumping a train. We started walking due east along the road as the first signs of dawn showed up ahead of us. It was bloody cold, I can tell you, but walking soon warmed us up. Chilla reckoned it was about nine miles into Parkes and he wanted to get there in time for breakfast. I wondered about that – we had nothing much with us, as all the money we had made out of the fight had gone on the kids. Chilla had his reserve fund, of course, but I knew he wouldn't spend that. But I had also learnt not to question old Chilla's plans.

On the way into town I asked Chilla why he hadn't waited for the bloke he'd helped into the wagon. He walked on, then, looking sideways at me, said, 'Snow, in his condition, and with that swag of his, we might have made it to town by midday. Experience is the best teacher, and if he followed us, it will be a lesson he won't forget.'

We got to Parkes a bit after half past seven and looked for a camp down on Goobang Creek, a tributary of the Lachlan. There was a camp of over twenty blokes in one spot. Chilla said good day to them, and then went on a hundred yards or so and threw his swag down under a shady tree. There was a good place to dip water, and I was about to fill the billy when Chilla stopped me.

'Don't worry about that, Snow, I think we'll try our luck up town.'

It would have been shorter to walk straight up, but Chilla went back past the big camp. There were some blokes he knew there, and they talked for a while about the state of the nation. One of the unemployed blokes who he called Jim was pretty bitter about it all.

It was quite a long walk to the town, and once there, we strolled along one of the main streets until we were outside a big cafe. Chilla looked it over.

'This will do. Let's get a decent feed into us.'

As we walked in, the large Italian proprietor greeted us a little warily.

Chilla walked on and we sat down at a table right at the back.

'Never sit near the front door,' Chilla advised me. 'It makes the cafe owner nervous in times like this.'

He ignored the menu on the table and, when the waitress came over, ordered two large mixed grills. They were huge meals and the best I've ever tasted – steak, bacon, chops, sausages and eggs piled on a huge platter. We got stuck into them, I can tell you. I noticed Chilla had his tobacco and matches beside his plate. Christ, I thought to myself, he's going to pull the fly trick. Sure enough, he'd almost finished when in went the flies.

'Excuse me, Miss,' he said as the waitress passed, 'there's flies in my food.'

The girl gave a gasp of horror and ran over to the boss.

Over he came. 'Watsa matter? watsa matter?'

Chilla, who now had his wallet in his hand as though ready to pay, made a retching sound and pointed to his plate. 'Flies! There's flies in my food.'

'No fly, no fly, thisa d'clean aplace,' cried the Italian.

'Well, what are those, kite hawks?' Chilla made a retching sound again.

'Oright, oright, you no pay, ona d'house, ona d'house, oright.'

Wringing his hands, the outwitted Italian returned to his cash register.

Chilla rolled a smoke, lit it and leaned back in his chair.

'Very generous people, the Italians,' he said. 'Good cooks, too . . . A bit unsteady under fire, though,' he added thoughtfully, blowing smoke towards the ceiling. I almost laughed – Chilla's opinion of all nationalities was largely based on the performance of the army during the Great War. We had another drink of tea and, nodding our thanks to the cafe owner, we left.

'Well, Snow,' said my mate, letting his belt out a hole 'that was a bloody good feed, I'm as full as a butcher's pup.'

As we strolled back to camp, we passed a small house. The name O'Reilly could be seen in faded writing on the letterbox.

By the side of the house an old woman was vainly trying to clear the overgrown yard with a hoe. Chilla stopped short, opened the rickety gate, and walked in. I noticed he had developed his limp. He took off his hat and said, 'Good morning, Lady.'

The old girl looked up. 'Clear out, you'll get no handouts here.'

'Of course not,' said Chilla. 'We don't want anything. I just couldn't help coming in to say hello, you look so much like my dear mother, God rest her soul.' Chilla crossed himself with a flourish. 'My name is O'Rourke, and this is Snowy Wilson, a young chap I've befriended.'

The old lady still looked uncertain. 'I saw you limping. Were you in the war?'

'Yes, wounded on the Somme, but they patched me up and sent me back to the front.'

The old lady's face softened. 'I lost my only son on the Somme.'

'I'm sorry,' Chilla said, and for all his palaver, I knew he meant it. He stepped forward and gently took the hoe from her. 'Please, let us give you a hand. It will be our good deed for the day. I only wish I'd been able to do more for my poor mother before she passed away.'

I thought he was going to cross himself again, but old Chilla never overdid things. Anyway, to make a long story short, we got stuck in and cleaned up the old girl's yard for her. Later she sat us down at the kitchen table for a lunch of tea and mutton sandwiches. She apologised for the state of the garden, saying she had been in hospital.

Chilla made sympathetic noises and told her what excellent mutton she had. She was curious about the war and Chilla talked more to her about it than to anyone I knew. He never mentioned anything that would upset the old girl, though.

She got us another cup of tea and she and Chilla talked about the depression, and just about everything else as well. Listening to them, I was as bored as a bushman at a ballet. Finally, she looked at him and said, 'Are you on the dole?'

'No, Mrs O'Reilly, I'm not. You see, I like to be independent . . . and this young fellow,' he said, nodding at me, 'looks older than he is. Not long ago, he escaped from a brutal orphanage, and he's afraid of authority.'

The old lady tut-tutted at that bit of information and, getting up from the table, went over to her larder. 'I must give you something to take with you,' she said.

'No, no, you mustn't do that,' said Chilla, 'we're all right.'

'Perhaps you are, but I'm still going to give you something.' She rummaged around in a cupboard.

'I don't seem to have any clean bags, but you must accept some food.'

'Well, if you must,' Chilla said, 'I just happen to always carry a couple of tuckerbags with me.'

He pulled two clean pillowcases out of one inside coat pocket, and from another, two small calico bags. The old lady gave him a hard look, then chuckled. We went away with two flaps of mutton and some flour, as well as tea and sugar. She even threw in a couple of onions and a tin of baking powder. As we left, Chilla promised to return and fix up the front gate.

On the way back to camp I asked Chilla if we should have taken the food from the old girl. He stopped and looked at me.

'Yes, Snow, it was very important to her that we did. It wasn't for cleaning up the yard – it was for the company. You'll find most old people are terribly lonely. Once they realise you're not a threat to them, they'll talk the hind leg off a donkey. You see, Snow, we made that old lady happy, and that's worth a lot more than a bit of tucker.'

What he said made sense, but he did admit we'd had a very profitable day.

As we got to our camp on the creek, we saw that the train jumper had arrived, and had camped between us and the main group. We put the tucker away and were boiling the billy when he came over, looking exhausted. Chilla nodded to him, and asked him if he'd like a drink of tea.

'Yes, please. I tried to boil my billy, but it fell into the fire and put it out.'

'How the hell did that happen?'

'Well, I had it hanging on a stick, like I've seen in pictures, but the stick caught fire and the billy fell off.

'I wanted to experience life on the road – I'm a journalist. I don't think I'm up to it, though. My heels are blistered and my shoulder's chaffed from that swag.'

Chilla handed him a mug of tea. 'I don't bloody well wonder, humping a married man's swag like that. On the road, you have to travel light, you carry only the essentials. No one would employ a man with a swag like that.'

'Why not?'

'Well, in that kind of swag, you fall into a heavy, drugged sleep and you'd find it hard to wake up. A man should be comfortable in his swag, but just able to feel the cold. That way, you sleep lightly, wake up easily, and are alert straight away.'

The young bloke took a sip of tea and looked up at Chilla. 'Well, I'm not sure what I should carry. Would you mind coming over later and going through my gear?'

Chilla thought for a while. 'All right. As long as you're prepared to take advice.'

The young bloke nodded, and asked Chilla if he would teach him to boil the billy at the same time.

Half an hour after the young train jumper had departed, we went over to his camp. He had his swag unrolled and had his gear and clothing scattered around the flat like a dog's breakfast. There was a suit, town clothes, town shoes, and Christ knows what else. Chilla took one look at it all and shook his head.

'Right, pick out two pairs of working trousers, two shirts and three pairs of socks. Keep the overcoat, and give the rest away. Now, for your swag. How many blankets do you have?'

'Only three.'

'That's one too many. Get rid of one, and toss that pillow as well. Use your clothes instead. Now, let's have a look at your cooking gear.'

The young train jumper produced two billies, two small saucepans and a frypan. Chilla looked at him. 'Jesus Christ! It's a wonder you didn't bring a bloody horse and cart. Keep the two billies, if you like, but get rid of the rest.'

The young chap looked as though he'd been kicked in the guts, then he brightened up. 'I could send the stuff I don't want back to Sydney.'

'Yes, if you're flush with money, you could do that, and buy a waterbag and a solid pair of walking boots at the same time. As you look to have plenty of tucker, stay here until you've broken in both the bag and the boots. By then, your heels should be right.'

The young train jumper seemed a lot happier now he wasn't going to lose his belongings for good. He looked at Chilla. 'What about the right way to boil a billy?'

'Right, go and fill the smallest of those billies.'

Chilla got a fire going and showed him how to push the billy in to the edge of the fire so that the flames would lick around its sides.

'Always drop the handle away from the fire so you can pick it up,' he told the young fella.

'Now, this is a new billy and will take some time to boil, as the shiny surface reflects the heat. When it's older and blackened it will absorb heat better and boil quicker. I'm telling you these things because I don't like to see young chaps getting into trouble, so I hope you're bloody well taking notice.'

The young bloke said he was very grateful, and we sat around and smoked until the billy boiled.

'Right,' said Chilla, 'she's galloping. Where's your tea?'

The young bloke produced an unopened packet of tea and handed it to Chilla. He tore it open and threw half a handful of tea into the boiling water. He lifted the billy off by the handle and said, 'There you are, as simple as that. Now give me your tea bag.'

'What tea bag?'

'The bag to carry your tea in.'

'I'm sorry, I don't have one.'

'All right, then, give me one of those clean socks you were going to toss out.' Chilla took the packet of tea and, holding the open end up, he pushed it into the toe of the sock then knotted the sock above it.

'There, that will do until you get some bags. You'll need one for meat, and another three for flour, sugar and tea. The only tinned stuff you should carry is baking powder, to make dampers. I'd eat the tinned food you've got there before you leave here.'

We left him sorting his scattered belongings and returned to our own camp. Chilla knocked up a damper, while I cut up an onion and put one of the flaps on to boil in our biggest billy can. Chilla brought the damper dough over and buried it in coals and hot ash. As you'd know, Simmo, when you're cooking a damper in the coals, the dough has to be pretty stiff so it will retain its shape. Old Chilla was a past master at it.

I probably ate more tucker that day than on any other day during the depression.

Next day we went back up town and repaired the old lady's front gate. She greeted us like long lost relatives, and insisted on giving us a smoko of fresh baked scones. As we left, she made Chilla promise to keep in touch, and despite his protests, she saw us off with the remainder of the scones wrapped in a teatowel.

That afternoon, we were having a nap when one of the men from the big camp arrived. 'G'day, Chilla, how are you getting on in this land fit for heroes?'

'Oh, pretty well, Joe, considering.'

'Well, there's a lot of poor bastards not doing too well at all. I reckon something's got to be done about it. The bankers are running the bloody country and the families of returned men are starving.'

Chilla nodded. 'I know, Joe, the Labor Government has done nothing.'

'Nothing is right, they've sold us out. They've brought this German Jew out to tell us to tighten our belts – and we're on the bloody bread line.'

'I resent it as much as you, Joe, but he's an Englishman, actually, and a director of the Bank of England. He's only the bloody messenger.'

'Well, he sounds like a Jew. Anyway, I don't give a damn what he is, it's wrong. I've gone into this pretty thoroughly, Chilla. It's clear that Australia's being victimised; we ended up owing the Poms nearly a hundred million pounds in war loans and bonds. Now, if you don't know what for, I'll tell you – it was to keep the AIF in the field, fighting for bloody England. America reduced the rate on its loans to England by two per cent, other nations have been given relief – but not us. We lost over sixty thousand men in the war, and the bastards do this to us.'

Chilla scratched his head. 'No, it's not right, Joe. The bloody Bank of England seems to be running this country.

The way unemployed diggers have been treated is a bloody disgrace. I agree with everything you've said – but you've got to be realistic, if the politicians can't or won't stand up to the bankers, there's nothing you or I can do about it. It's no good flogging a dead horse. All you can do is look after number one. If you don't, no one else will.'

'Well, something has to be done about it. We've got a meeting over at the camp tonight. Come along and lend your support.'

'All right, we'll be there.'

After he'd gone, Chilla didn't say much, but after we'd had a feed that night, we went over to the big camp. They had a roaring fire going, and the group had grown since we first arrived. Joe told them who we were and then opened the proceedings by giving much the same spiel as he'd hit us with.

What followed was a lot of wild talk from some of the blokes about taking things into their own hands. Chilla had a few words to say, warning them that violence would achieve nothing. The only hope, he said, was to make sure Lang won the state election. At least that should improve things in New South Wales.

We stayed for an hour or so, then went back to our own camp. Chilla put the billy on for tea, and placed the other mutton flap in the big billy to cook overnight. That puzzled me a bit, as we hadn't eaten all the first one. We had a drink of tea, and after thinking for a while, Chilla looked at me over the top of his mug.

'We'll pack up and get away from here at daylight tomorrow morning,' he said.

'Why, what's wrong?' I asked him.

'I'd say the wallopers will be down here tomorrow to move that crowd on. I'll bet there was at least one police spy in that group.'

He was a wise old bird, Chilla, because afterwards we heard that that was exactly what happened.

Snowy sat up and yawned. 'Well, Simmo, I'm a working man. I'll see you in the morning.'

# 9

Next morning I got up with Snowy and gave him a hand with his yard work. By lunchtime most of the jobs were done. We had a meal, then a dinner camp, and at four o'clock I met him in the bar for a session. Snowy was still rather subdued, but after a few beers he livened up and became his usual loquacious self. As he leant on the bar, he looked at me sidewards. 'Did I ever tell you about the time old Chilla raffled my overcoat?'

I told him that was one I hadn't heard. 'Was it long after you both left Parkes?' I asked.

'No, you'll remember that we shot through after that meeting on Goobang Creek. Well, we got going before it was light and headed up the Peak Hill road. On the way out of town, we snavelled some vegetables from a Chinese garden: we got some carrots, a small cabbage and then bandicooted six potatoes.'

'You what?' I asked him . . .

We bandicooted six spuds. What you do is dig a hole and take one potato off each plant without disturbing it. When the holes are filled in, no one is any the wiser.

Old Chilla said that in the early days the Chinese had cleared most of the country around where we were. They had gone from gold mining to land clearing, then to market gardening. The Chinese, he said, were very industrious people who used human waste as fertiliser. The Chinese, I believe, didn't fire a shot in anger during the war, so he left it at that. Anyway, the vegetables tasted first rate.

We were lucky enough to pick up a bit of burr cutting around Peak Hill, then headed for Dubbo. There were a lot of blokes carrying their swags then. Most of them were on the dole – or sustenance, as some called it. The unemployed blokes got these food coupons from the coppers, which they would exchange for meat at the local butcher's and for rations at the stores. Just flour and tea and a few essentials, but no tobacco. The cops liked to see the unemployed keep moving, so, out bush, they had to tramp on to the next police station before they got the next week's dole. Chilla reckoned it was to prevent them becoming organised. There were plenty of agitators about, as the whole country was filled with unrest.

Chilla wouldn't go on 'susso', though; he was too independent. He reckoned he could live on his wits and put money in his pocket. He wasn't impressed by a lot of blokes who tried, though. He said if most of them attempted to live on their wits, they'd starve. After a couple of weeks, he reckoned, you'd be able to count their ribs through a flannel shirt at five paces.

Chilla always made sure he had money on him, so the coppers couldn't arrest him as a vagrant. There were plenty of keen young coppers out to make a name for themselves who gave the down and outs hell. Chilla always kept on the right side of publicans and police sergeants. Although, there were exceptions, of course. He said that sergeants ran the army and the police force, but he hated constables – bloody upstarts, he called them – reminded him of provos.

I was droving with Chilla once. On watch, he used to sing a song about provos. I remember most of it, if you'd like to hear it?

Snowy had a voice that is best described as a barbed wire baritone. I declined as gracefully as possible, saying I'd rather hear some more of Chilla's exploits.

Right, well, as I said before, things were bloody tough then. There was a lot of door-to-door selling. Even the big drug firms had vans on the road selling patent medicine. Chilla used to say that they sold stuff that would cure anything from coughs and colds to sore holes and pimples on the dick. There were blokes going around doing up saws for farmers and others sharpening scissors for the womenfolk. There were blokes selling everything from clothes props to safety pins. I think Chilla used to feel sorry for a lot of them. 'Snowy,' he would say, 'most of these poor bastards couldn't sell rafts at a shipwreck, but at least they're having a go.' He used to get a bit depressed at times, old Chilla did. 'As sure as there's dung in a goose,' he'd say, 'if something isn't done soon, this country will go communist.'

'He wasn't a commo, though, was he?'

'No, I don't think so. He just got upset to see blokes who had been through hell in the war reduced to begging ...

I remember one Anzac day he and I watched the march. Old Chilla never marched himself, and I never saw him wear a medal. Anyway, we watched the returned blokes march past in down-at-heel boots, with their returned soldier's badges pinned on tattered unpressed coats. Chilla just stood there, he never made a sound, but the tears were running down his face. Afterwards he went away on his own and got as drunk as I've ever seen him.

No, I'm sure he wasn't a commo. Later he sometimes used to talk about a thing called Douglas Credit, in some country called Alberta. At least, I think that was its name. Chilla reckoned that might be the answer. He also told me that Jack Lang had some of the same ideas.

Old Chilla didn't stay depressed for long, though. He soon thought up some cunning way of getting a quid and was on top of the world again.

Anyway, to get back to this yarn – we knocked around for a while, picking up a bit of sucker bashing between Dubbo and Coonabarabran. You'd know what that is?

'Yes, Snow. I've had a go at it.'

Well, the hungry bastard who owned the place paid us two and six an acre. I think that was the going price, but the regrowth was so thick a dog couldn't bark in the bloody place. He gave us a tent that you could see through, two blunt axes and a rusty file that was as blunt as the axes. He promised to give us free mutton, but it turned out that the sheep it had come from must have died of old age. Anyway, we set up camp at a waterhole on the edge of this 30 acres of previously ringbarked country, then looked without enthusiasm at the thicket in front of us. Chilla pushed his hat back and scratched his head.

'I wondered why this job hadn't been snapped up, with so many out of work. Now I know.'

As you'd know, you don't need a razor-sharp axe to knock suckers off, but the axes we had were bloody hopeless. The owner of the place had given us some rations – to be paid for later, of course – so while I made a stew out of the ram stag mutton, Chilla took the axes down to the waterhole. Chilla was a bloke who always had an answer to everything.

I wandered down when I got the stew cooking, to see what he was up to. I found him grinding the axe blades down on a large, flat stone on the edge of the water. By the time the stew was cooked, the sun was down, and Chilla had the axes reasonably sharp.

Snowy paused to roll a smoke. I wondered when the overcoat was going to enter the yarn, but Snowy was not one to be sidetracked. He lit the cigarette and continued.

At the end of the first day, we had done over two acres, and my hands were red raw with broken blisters. Chilla inspected them, and taking out his pocketknife, cut off the loose tops of the blisters.

'Now, go and piss on them, and do that every time you want a leak. You'll find they'll be right in no time.'

I followed his advice. Using the axe was still hell, but in a few days time my hands hardened up. In the meantime, Chilla took over the cooking – he reckoned the mutton could do with a bit of seasoning, but not that particular flavour. After a week we had the job about half done and Chilla said it was time to improve our diet.

There were some fat wethers in the next paddock, watering just below the hole we were camped on. Chilla reckoned they had been missed during the last shearing, as most of them were almost wool blind. The next afternoon, taking one of the axes with us, we went down to the hole while they were still camped there.

Creeping up on them, Chilla seized a likely-looking wether and cut its throat with his trusty pocketknife. Feeling the butt of its tail, he grinned. 'Prime, Snow, bloody prime.'

He set about skinning the carcass, leaving the head and legs below the knees and hocks still attached. I gathered some bushes to put the mutton on while Chilla did the butchering. He used the axe to cut off the ribs. When he had finished, he pushed the guts back into the skin and, using his pocketknife as an awl, sewed it up with a bit of tie wire he'd removed from the fence.

'Now, Snow,' he said, standing back and admiring his handiwork, 'this wether came down to have a drink, and his fleece being so heavy, the poor bastard drowned. Lend a hand and we'll launch him.'

We took the carcass down to the hole and heaved it out into deeper water. Then we carried the mutton back to the camp and spread it out on some bushes. We covered it up as best we could – the weather was still cold, so the flies were not a great worry.

There had been a camp at the end of the hole we were on, and while Chilla broke up the chops with the axe, I wandered over to see what I could find. There was not a lot to see, but after searching the place thoroughly I went back to our camp with a partly flattened kerosene tin. Chilla gave it a quick once over.

'Good work, Snow. Flatten it out properly with the other axe and we've got a top notch griller.'

I was wondering how we were going to cook the legs of mutton, but as we sat around smoking after devouring the chops, Chilla explained. 'Now, Snow, I want you to go along the creek and pick up as many flat stones as you can find, up to twelve inches across.'

I hunted around, and before dark I had twelve of the stones he wanted. When I got back I found Chilla had dug a hole and had a large fire going. He lined the hole with the stones, and when the fire had died down a bit, he transferred a lot of it to the hole. Half an hour later he raked all but a few coals and hot ash out. The stones were by then as hot as hell. Chilla then put some leaves in the bottom and placed a leg of mutton in the hole. To complete the oven, he placed the tin grill over the hole and piled coals on top.

'By morning,' Chilla told me, 'that leg will be food for the Gods.'

He was right, and for the remainder of the job we lived like fighting cocks. The owner came out a couple of days later to see how we were going. Chilla told him the job would be finished at the end of the week, and said he could pick us up then.

As it was midday Chilla invited him to have a feed. He was handed a slab of damper laden with prime mutton. The cocky gave it a hard look and chewed it thoughtfully, but he didn't say anything.

We cleared three quid out of the sucker bashing – a lot better than the dole, but we earned every penny. We were happy enough, though, for all wages had been cut by ten per cent. Of course, tucker was pretty cheap those days. Meat was about sixpence a pound, you could buy a loaf of bread for under a zack, and syrup was also about a zack a tin.

We got to Coonabarabran in the middle of a late cold snap with sleety rain. The first thing I did was to go into a shop and buy a Tasmanian bluey overcoat. It cost all of my money from the sucker bashing, but I reckoned it was grouse. Chilla nearly had a fit when he saw it back at our camp on the banks of the Castlereagh.

'Snowy, my lad,' he said sadly, 'I don't think I'll ever rear you; however, we must find a way to turn your extravagance into financial gain.'

The next morning Chilla was up early and whistling about the camp. I knew for sure he had thought up some cunning scheme – and I was not mistaken. After breakfast he put me in the picture.

'It's Saturday today, Snow, and a lot of country people will be in town. About midday I want you to go up town and find the top pub. Leave that coat of yours with me and wear the thinnest clobber you have. When you're at the pub, order the cheapest drink, and make a big thing out of finding the money to pay for it. Shiver a bit, if you can. I'll be in a bit later.'

I had no idea what Chilla was up to, but knew that there would be money in it somewhere. About twelve o'clock I went up to the town, cursing Chilla as I walked. A bitterly cold wind made a joke of his advice to try and shiver a bit. I picked out the most posh pub and went in with teeth chattering, and almost blue with the cold. There was a fire going in the bar, but as that area was already crowded, I crept into a corner. I ordered a half rum, and my fumbling to get the money out of my pocket with frozen fingers was no act.

I sipped the rum slowly, and twenty minutes later, Chilla strolled into the bar with my overcoat over his arm. He looked around and announced in a loud voice:

'Righto, gents, here's your chance to get a brand new Tasmanian bluey for next to nothing.'

Somehow or other, Chilla's presence always seemed to demand respect, but one cocky young bloke said, 'Come on, what's the catch?'

'This is no con,' said my mate. 'My mother is very ill in Sydney. I'm going to raffle this coat to try and raise my fare to see her. Only a zack a ticket. Now, you can't beat that – a brand new coat for sixpence. We'll draw it here in a minute or two.'

Within seconds Chilla had pulled a book of raffle tickets out of his pocket and was doing a roaring trade. He finally came to where I was shivering in the corner.

'Right, sonny, you look as though you could do with a decent coat. Only a zack a ticket.'

He gave me the wink and I knew what to do. I delved around in my pocket and stammered I-I do-don't th-think.

The publican, who was standing by, said, 'Here, I'll put him in the draw.'

Chilla took the zack and looked at me. 'What's your name, sonny?'

Mine was the last ticket to go into Chilla's hat. He gave it a good shake to mix up the tickets, then asked, 'Now, who will we get to draw out the winner?'

A chorus of voices answered him. 'The barmaid, the barmaid.'

'Right,' said Chilla, then, holding the hat up, he leaned over the bar. The girl took out a ticket and looked at it closely. She handed it back to Chilla. 'I think it says Snowy.'

Chilla examined the ticket. 'Yes, that's it. Is there a Snowy in the bar?'

I put my hand up. 'Th-that's m-my na-name,' I said through chattering teeth. Chilla handed me my coat amid loud applause. The publican came over to us.

'I don't drink myself,' Chilla told him, 'but I'd like to buy this young man a drink.'

I thanked him, and told the publican I'd have a full rum. I bloody well needed it, I can tell you. I had no idea how Chilla had worked the raffle, but it was not the last time he raffled my Tasmanian bluey. And I was always the winner.

As soon as the weather warmed up a bit, he told me to keep it in my swag. Anyway, that day we left the hotel together in high spirits. On the way back to camp, we called in at the butcher's shop and bought a piece of silverside. Now the raffle was over, Chilla said we could be seen together. He was a funny sort of bloke, a real con man at times, although he never touched a battler. At other times he would give you the shirt off his back.

Chilla always had with him what he called his tools of trade. A set of dice, a pack of cards, three Edward the Seventh pennies for two-up, and a couple of cheap books of raffle tickets. These things were illegal gaming equipment and you could be arrested if they were found in your possession. Old Chilla was too cunning to get caught, though. He had a beautiful big bible he kept in his swag – when I first saw it I asked him if it was his family bible. He laughed and said it was a smuggler's bible he'd bought at a Paddington hock shop. A block of middle pages had been cut away, leaving a hidden chamber. It was in there that Chilla kept his gambling gear. He had it well padded so nothing rattled, and out of his head he had written up family details in the front. A red ribbon was always tied round the bible.

As Chilla's mother was supposed to be dying in Sydney, we decided to move on the next day. We carried our swags towards Gunnedah and camped a couple of days on Coxs Creek. Chilla produced a fishing line from his swag and we tried our luck. That swag of old Chilla's was as thin as the seat of a politician's pants, but what he could produce from it was bloody amazing. Anyway, we caught a feed or two of fish and moved on. When we got to Gunnedah we camped a bit out of town on the Namoi. We had heard there was a camp of unemployed at the showgrounds, but Chilla liked to be out of the limelight. We went into town by separate routes and Chilla pulled the overcoat rort again. The weather had warmed up quite a bit, so the response wasn't as good, but Chilla was happy.

The state elections were to be held the following Saturday. Lang was promising to stop the forced sale of property by mortgagees, and was going to bail up on paying interest on overseas loans. According to everyone, he looked a certain winner.

There was a number of pubs in the town, and one of them was run by a relieving manager, a bit of a standover merchant. They reckoned he was an ex-copper, and he was one of the few publicans Chilla disliked. One day we heard that this publican had given a hiding to an unemployed bloke who had asked for a handout. Back in camp Chilla was very quiet, then 'Snowy,' he said, 'I think we should pay this bastard a visit. We'll have a look around his premises tonight when all honest men are asleep.'

Well, we did that, not that there was much to see – the usual toilets, a carbide gas generator for the lights, a well stocked wood heap and a fowl run. Chilla seemed satisfied, though, and whistled to himself on the way back to camp. Over a drink of tea, he looked at me. He had a gleam in his eye that I knew meant trouble for the publican.

'On Saturday night, Snow, we'll run a few raffles in our friend's public bar. I've heard he and his wife always play bowls on Saturdays and stay for the social. There'll be no problem with the sergeant, I've known him for a while.'

I asked him what the hell he was going to raffle.

'Snowy,' he said, 'the solution to a problem is usually found within the problem itself.'

I hadn't any bloody idea what he was talking about, of course, but he was like that. He reckoned you learnt more if you had to work things out for yourself.

'Well,' I asked, 'who's going to get the dough?'

'Ah,' he said, 'that's a good question. It will be for charity, of course, the relief fund for unemployed workers.'

On Saturday there was a stock sale on, bringing plenty of country people into town. As soon as we had a bit of breakfast Chilla scratched his chin and said, 'Pack up and roll your swag. I think it may be better if we're somewhere else tomorrow.'

Later we strolled up town. Chilla led the way to the showground where he had heard the unemployed group was camped. True enough, there were about twenty men sitting around behind the grandstand. The bloke who had been knocked about by the publican was lying on his swag. Chilla walked up and looked them over.

'Have you chaps got a spokesman?'

No one said a word, then a bloke who had been sitting with his head in his hands looked up.

'Ah, it's you, O'Rourke. I thought I recognised the voice.'

Chilla walked over to him and spoke quietly. 'Yes, Sir, it's me. I'd like you to do something for me. On Monday morning there will be some food delivered here. Could you take control and see it's distributed fairly?'

The man stood up and just for a moment he looked like a different person. He shook hands with Chilla.

'Leave it in my hands, and thank you.'

As we walked away from the showground I sorta felt that Chilla had done more than just give a job to the man he had called Sir. I never asked Chilla who he was, and Chilla never said, but I think he must have been an officer Chilla had known in the war. When we got to town Chilla went to the butcher's shop, where he paid for twenty-five pounds of sausages and five pounds of dripping to be delivered to the showgrounds on Monday morning. We then went to the bakers, and he paid for a dozen loaves of bread to be delivered to the same place. I thought it was a bit risky spending the money before the raffle, but I'd learnt never to question old Chilla.

That afternoon we strolled into the pub we had targeted. Chilla explained to the barmaids that we had permission to run a charity raffle and would like to hold it in the bar that night about eight o'clock. Permission was granted and it was suggested that half past seven would be a better time. Chilla agreed. We had a couple of beers, then walked up to a store that sold just about everything. Chilla bought six cheap calico marble bags with drawstrings and a bottle of black ink, then we headed back to the camp. Chilla whistled and occasionally chuckled to himself on the way.

Once in the camp Chilla poured the ink into an empty Turk's Head coffee tin and topped it up with water. Then he put the marble bags into this brew to soak and told me to put the billy on – we'd left enough gear out to make a drink of tea.

Chilla's mood had changed a bit by then. He took a sip of tea and growled.

'You know, Snow, I'd like to have that bastard's guts for garters, but a raffle will have to do. When we go up town later, we'll take our swags with us.'

A bit before half past seven we headed up town and left our gear and swags at the railway line. It was quite dark by then. Chilla didn't go into the bar at the hotel but slipped around the back. He beckoned to me and I followed him into the fowl yard. All the fowls were asleep, and what he did next has always amazed me. Taking one of the dyed bags out of his pocket, he slipped it quickly over a sleeping chook's head.

Telling me to watch carefully, he captured another. The fowls seemed to be completely stunned by it. Chilla turned to me.

'Right, Snow, your turn. Get one more. You'll have to keep the supply up to me later when I start the raffles.'

I got the third chook, and I couldn't believe it was so easy. Chilla handed me one of his and, taking the other, walked through the front door and announced:

'Righto, fellas, here we are – chook raffle sixpence a ticket. Proceeds go to the fund for the relief of the unemployed.'

I reckon old Chilla could sell ice boxes to the Eskimos, for the whole thing went so smoothly you wouldn't bloody well believe it. As Chilla was raffling one chook, I was knocking off the next one from the chook house. After we'd done eight, Chilla closed the proceedings down. We had a couple of beers, thanked the girls, then walked up to the station and caught the last goods train out of town.

# 10

Snowy and I were the only ones in the bar. The publican polished the bar down to where we were and shouted us both a drink. He had one himself and stayed to hear another of Snowy's yarns.

My mate said good luck to the publican, and after wiping the froth off his top lip, he turned to me.

'Did I ever tell you about the time Chilla and I shore sheep for nothing?'

I assured him I hadn't, so taking another swig, he got into full stride.

> Well, after Chilla took a rise out of that publican we headed back out west. Lang had won the state election, but things were in a bloody mess, just the same. Chilla reckoned Scullin was as weak as piss. According to him, the prime minister had gone overseas for a long trip, leaving the country in the hands of the bankers – who, he said, were following orders from England. With Theodore out of the picture, they had an open slather.
>
> Anyway, to get back to this story. We picked up a job or two here and there for a few days, and Chilla ran a swy game – you know, two-up – when he got the chance. We got by all right, but it was no picnic, I can tell you. We spent Christmas on the banks of Gunningbar Creek, and had a feed of rabbit and johnny cakes. That was more than a lot of poor bastards ate for Christmas dinner.

Snowy stopped and drained his glass. He looked at the publican. 'Fill 'em up again, boss.'

As the publican was refilling our glasses, I asked Snowy if he ever got sick of eating rabbits.

'Too bloody right we did, but when you've got the arse out of your pants, you can't afford to be fussy. Mind you, they weren't too bad, and a great standby.'

The publican returned with three beers. Snowy gave the collar on his beer a long look. He didn't say anything, but the publican topped it up. Snowy took a long swallow and continued.

Well, in January Chilla and I picked up a bit of council relief work at Nyngan. There was a bit of a blue on about the rate of pay. When Chilla found out that the scheme was undercutting the award wage, he jacked up, and, of course, I left with him. We found a good camp down on the Bogan and tried our hand at fishing. There was a group of blokes who were humping their swags camped there as well. They had just tramped in and were waiting to pick up the dole at Nyngan. They weren't a happy bunch, I can tell you. Those days when men got together the talk was pretty revolutionary. We were all sitting around the fire one night, when one of the unemployed blokes said he'd had enough.

'We should raise the Eureka flag, march on Canberra and show those bastards how to run the country.'

Chilla looked at him. 'You're talking rebellion, you know.'

'My bloody oath I am.'

'Well, you can go your hardest, but I've done all the marching and fighting I want to do.'

'That's all right, we can do without gutless wonders.'

Without speaking, Chilla picked him up by the shirt and knocked him clean over the fire.

We shifted camp next day and humped our swags up the Bogan towards Buddabadah. There had been an early flood in the river and a lot of the fences were down. We were lucky enough to pick up a few weeks work repairing them. The wage was two pound six a week, and keep. Youth wages were only nineteen and six, but I was going on for seventeen and a hefty lad, so I got the full wage.

Later we got a job burr cutting with a gang near Warren. The wages were the same, from memory, but we had to put in two bob a week each for butter. I didn't mind that, I was on full wages, and I hadn't tasted butter for a bloody long time. We were cutting Bathurst burr and Paterson's curse, both of them bloody menaces. There was a South Australian in the gang, who for some reason that I've never worked out was called 'Yarra'. The funny thing was that he said Paterson's curse was a garden plant in South Australia, called Salvation Jane. These bloody burrs got into the fleeces of sheep and made shearing dangerous. The cutters could jam on the burrs, and the shearers could lose control of the hand pieces. A runaway hand piece is bloody deadly.

I bought a round of drinks, and in the pause I asked Snowy about Noogoora Burr.

'No, Simmo, like prickly pear, it was never a problem in New South Wales. They both came over the border in places, but neither were the menace they were here in Queensland.'

Anyway, to get back to the yarn. This Yarra was a moody sort of bloke. One night we were sitting around yarning, when someone said that Dame Nellie Melba had died. Yarra spat in the fire and growled.

'I'll bet a dole chit to a dud cheque she didn't die of hunger.'

Someone chipped him. 'That's not a very nice thing to say. She was a great Australian.'

'Maybe she was, but it's the truth, and the truth is often unpleasant.'

More and more workers and unemployed had had a gutful of the depression. Lang had passed his bill to prevent forced sales and was threatening to stop paying the interest on overseas loans. According to Chilla, he planned to raise money, ignoring the gold standard. This gold standard, I believe, was a bit of a sacred cow those days. Apparently he thought the unemployed were more important than debts. But Chilla reckoned the banks would beat him in the end. The Government in Canberra, according to my mate, was up a well known creek without a paddle. Theodore had been reinstated as treasurer, but Lyons, who had filled his shoes in his absence, was leading a rebellious group.

The country was in a bloody mess all right. Wool had dropped from twenty-five pounds a bale to a little over eight pounds a bale. Wheat, they reckoned, had fallen over fifty per cent a bushel. As a result, the smaller woolgrowers and farmers were having a battle to survive. The thirty per cent cut in the shearing rates had been passed, and shed hands wages were slashed as well. The whole wool industry was in bloody turmoil. Later, when we were on the track, we heard a rumour that a breakaway union called the Pastoral Workers Industrial Union was being formed. It was a blood and guts group that played merry hell. The authorities reacted by arresting strikers under an old English law, and that just added insult to injury.

Snowy stopped and drained his glass. 'Your shout, boss,' he told the publican, and rolled a smoke.

The publican came back, shaking his head.

'How do you remember all this detail?'

I grinned. 'I've asked him the same question.'

'Well, I do remember most of it, and I cut bits out of the papers during the depression... One time,' he added rather shamefaced, 'I was going to write a bloody book. I even took a correspondence course and did the research.'

'Why the hell didn't you do it?' I asked him.

'Oh, it all seemed so bloody complicated, and, as you know, I'm not even much of a letter writer. Anyway, do you blokes want to hear the rest of this story?'

We told him we did and he settled down again.

Right, where was I? Well, after we left the burr cutting gang, we headed down towards Trundle. For the next two or three months Chilla and I knocked about the central west of New South Wales. Late in April we were on a road that followed the Lachlan. It was a good track with plenty of water and good camping spots.

We were getting by all right, but things had gone to the dogs in New South Wales. Lang, as he had promised, had put the unemployed before the payment of interest on overseas loans. This caused a hell of a stir and Scullin ended up making the payments for New South Wales. It's a sad fact of life, Simmo, that people always think of their hip pockets. Talk of doom by Lang's opponents caused a run on the State Savings Bank. It went bust and thousands of poor bastards lost their life's savings. Of course, they blamed Lang, and it did him a lot of harm politically.

Anyway, one midday we stopped for a bite to eat under a shady tree near a gate. The road we were travelling was a pretty rough dirt one. We were having a bit of a camp, when a buckboard approached from behind us. I opened the gate to let it through, and noticed that the driver was a woman. I also noticed that the single horse pulling the vehicle was lame.

Chilla was onto that like a flash. As I shut the gate, I heard him say, 'Missus, do you know you are driving a lame horse?'

The woman looked down at him.

'I know,' she said defensively. 'She needs shoeing, she's sore footed.'

'Well,' said Chilla, 'why doesn't your husband put some shoes on her?'

'My husband happens to be dead,' the woman said in a sharp voice. 'I can't shoe, but I don't see what business it is of yours.'

I had been summing up this woman while she and Chilla were talking. I reckon she was on the wrong side of forty. She was clean, but shabbily dressed, and had a kid of about three sitting next to her. Her reply had sat Chilla back a bit, I thought, but he rose to the occasion.

Chilla took off his hat. 'I'm sorry, missus, I just don't like to see a horse in trouble. I'll tell you what, if you give my mate and me a lift to your place, I'll shoe her for you.'

'That's very kind of you,' the woman said, 'but I can't afford to pay you.'

I thought Chilla had met his match, but no, he thought for a while, then said, 'Well, if you can give my mate and me a feed and somewhere to camp, we'll call it square.'

The woman looked from Chilla to the mare. She nodded her head, and told us to climb in the back seat.

It was no more than three miles to the woman's sheep farm. As I opened the gate I noticed the swaggies's code sign for 'too poor' scrawled on it. The place was pretty run down. The only reasonable building was a small two-stand shearing shed. We threw our swags in there and Chilla, after finding a set of horseshoes, proceeded with noticeable skill to shoe the buggy horse.

By the time he had finished, the sun was down. The woman sent a skinny girl of about nine out to tell us tea was ready. She showed us where to have a wash at a well in the yard.

The house needed painting, and I noticed the back door was almost off its hinges. We sat down at the table to a generous meal, though. It was roast rabbit and vegetables, but was well cooked. The vegetables were obviously home grown. The house was clean, but you could see signs of poverty everywhere. The woman had introduced herself as Mrs Schultz. Chilla complimented her on the meal and asked her about the vegetables.

You could see she was pleased, and she told us how she grew them herself and tried to be self supporting with chooks and her own milk and butter. She went on to tell us how hard it had been since her husband had died, and how she was trying to keep the place going, as well as giving the kids correspondence lessons. She told us of the plans she and her husband had once had for the place and how she wanted to hang on to it for the kids' sake. There were three children sitting around the table, watching us with eyes like saucers: a boy of about seven, the girl who had called us in to eat, and the tot who had been in the buckboard. Their mother changed the subject then and asked us a bit about ourselves.

Chilla answered her questions in a guarded way, then he asked her how long her husband had been dead. Just on three years, she told him. It was then that I opened my big mouth. I suppose knocking round with Chilla had made me blame most problems on the war. Anyway, I asked her if her husband had died of war wounds.

She gave me a hard look, and in a bitter kind of way replied, 'No, he died of blood poisoning. My husband was born in Germany, he tried to enlist, but they wouldn't take him. He could never understand why. He loved this country, and this place.' She looked at Chilla and spoke abruptly, 'I suppose you're a returned man?'

Chilla nodded. 'Yes, I am, but I don't think any the less of your husband for that. He must have been a good man.'

Chilla looked at the kids. 'You should always be proud of your dad,' he said, and he sorta spoke real gentle. I never heard Chilla speak like that before. He was a queer bird, old Chilla.

Anyway, this Mrs Schultz thaws out a bit after that. I reckon she never had no one to tell her troubles to since her old man died. She said the bank was giving her a hard time about the mortgage. She didn't say any more about it, but Chilla kept on about it, and finally she told us the story. The bank had written to her advising that a large amount had to be paid to reduce the mortgage within two months. If this payment wasn't made, the bank would foreclose and sell the property.

She said it was only a small place, but that there were about four thousand sheep ready to be shorn. She had asked the bank to advance enough money to pay for the shearing, but they had refused.

'So, that's the situation, I could pay the bank when I sell the wool, but I've no money to pay shearers.'

Chilla pushed back his chair. 'That's typical of banks. They seem hell bent on breaking this country, and everyone in it. You can't blame the managers, they're only following orders. They've been told to turn the screws.'

Chilla stopped talking, and Mrs Schultz said she was sorry to have loaded us with her problems. Chilla said it was all right, then he told her we had better get a good night's rest, as we had to move on in the morning.

We unrolled our swags and settled down for a smoke. There was something bothering me, though. I said to Chilla it was pretty stupid for a bank that wanted its money to stop the woman from being able to pay it. Chilla looked at me and told me I had a lot to learn.

'The bloody bank will grab the property. That way, they get the whole wool clip, plus the place.

'I lost a lot of good mates fighting the Germans, but I reckon the bloody banks are a bigger threat to this country than the Germans ever were.'

Chilla used to get a bit wound up at times, I reckon he liked to see people get a fair go. He was real stirred up about the banks.

I got up at daylight next morning, but Chilla was already up. I found him looking at the sheep yards.

'I reckon the good lady will have to spend some money on these yards before she can shear,' he said thoughtfully.

We could see Mrs Schultz had just finished milking up at the cow yard. We wandered up and said good morning to her.

I was admiring the Illawarra milkers, when I heard Chilla say, 'Is there any chance of breakfast before we leave?'

I had to admire the old bugger's cheek.

Mrs Schultz looked doubtful for a moment. 'Oh, all right,' she said, 'I've got plenty of eggs. Come on up to the house in half an hour.'

I wondered what Chilla was up to. I thought we were going to get an early start.

A little later we sat down to a breakfast of scrambled eggs and toasted homemade bread. When he had finished, Chilla pushed back his chair and spoke slowly, 'Have you tried to get shearers by payment with postdated cheques?'

Mrs Schultz laughed, but there was no humour in it. 'No one will touch a cheque of mine, postdated or not. The word is out that the bank will sell me up.'

Chilla thought for a moment. 'Those yards need a bit of work done on them before shearing.'

'So do a lot of other things. But I can't print money.'

Chilla scratched his head. 'No, you can't, but you can write out a postdated cheque for me and Snow. We'll do the shearing.'

The woman looked at him in disbelief. 'You must be mad.'

Chilla grinned at her. 'No, I just don't like to see banks getting away with murder.'

It was settled, then – and we went over to the yards to start the repairs. When we got there, I told him I thought the woman was right, he was bloody mad. Chilla looked at me and laughed. 'A bit of hard work never hurt anyone,' he said, 'and she is a damn good cook.'

We had the yard shipshape by lunchtime, and in the afternoon we mustered the sheep into the home paddock. After putting about a hundred and fifty into the shearing yards, we called it a day.

The change in our employer was something to see. As we went up for the evening meal, I heard her singing. I thought that Chilla may have fallen for her, and told him so. He thought that was a great joke and told me he had been up too many dry gullies to fall for a destitute widow with a debt-ridden property.

Next morning Chilla and me got stuck into the shearing. Chilla got the small motor that drove the overhead gear going, and started shearing the sheep. I penned up, picked up the fleeces and cleaned the dags and locks off. I then left the fleeces along the wall. After Chilla had shorn a dozen or so, he came over and did the classing. He seemed pretty impressed with the wool, saying they were good quality fine Merino fleeces, and showed me what to look for.

By four p.m. we had put through eighty sheep. Chilla stopped shearing and did the wool pressing, while I saddled a horse and took the shorn sheep out to another paddock.

The next day we managed to shear the rest of the sheep in the yards. Chilla gave me a go at classing, and after a while, reckoned I was good enough to do the job.

I had to admire that Mrs Schultz. She supervised the school work for the two eldest kids; she made butter and boiled up her own soap; she grew vegetables and made

*Next morning Chilla and me got stuck into the shearing.*

bread; and she looked after fences and kept the place in fair shape. She was also, as Chilla said, a damn good cook.

On the second day, Mrs Schultz came over to the shearing shed. We wondered what she wanted, but she ignored us, went into the shorn sheep pen and dragged a wether over to a nearby gallows. From the way she butchered that sheep, we could see it wasn't the first time she'd done it. From then on, she saddled a horse and kept the sheep up to us.

We worked seven days a week, and we worked bloody hard. Every night we went back and pressed the day's wool by the light of a hurricane light. We slept the sleep of the just – at least, that's what Chilla said – and we ate bloody good meals.

At the end of five weeks, Chilla pushed the last sheep down the let-go shute and stood back. 'Well, that's that. Let's get the pressing done and tidy up a bit.'

When we finished the pressing, there were over a hundred and thirty bales of high quality wool in the shed. That night the evening meal was a bit of a celebration. Mrs Schultz produced some home-brewed ginger beer, and apologised for not having anything stronger. After the plates were cleared away, she wrote out a cheque and handed it to Chilla.

Chilla looked up in surprise. 'This is very generous.'

'I don't think so. I owe you both more than I could ever pay – I can now give the bank their money and have enough to carry on.'

We said our goodbyes that night, and next morning we were on the track again. In the middle of the day we boiled up the billy under the shade of an old gum tree. As we sat and smoked, Chilla pulled the cheque out of his pocket. I was a bit curious about that cheque and asked him how much it was for. He looked at the cheque, then at me.

'Snowy,' he said, 'this cheque is for more than she can afford.' Then slowly he tore the cheque in half and threw the pieces into the fire.

As I've said before, he was a queer bird, old Chilla. I wasn't too worried about him burning the cheque, despite having done a fair bit myself to earn it. After all, we had lived on the best for over a month, and to do that in the middle of the depression was something to write home about.

Later in the year Chilla and I were camped near a little town on the Gwydir River, near Moree in New South Wales. It was a top camp on a billabong, and with us were two other blokes. One came from a town in Victoria called Wonthaggi, the other was a long streak from West Australia called Splinter. They were both good blokes and pulled their weight in the camp. Like Chilla, they weren't on sustenance, and that's probably why we all got on so well.

During June and July the Government opened the possum season to the unemployed. The pelts were at their best at that time of the year, and the country was lousy with grey brush-tail possums. As each skin brought three bob, it was fairly easy money. Chilla and I and the long bloke went into Moree and bought pliers, two rolls of piano wire and two light axes. We were ready to try our hands at possuming.

This Splinter was the thinnest man I've ever struck – over six feet and under ten stone. Chilla reckoned he'd have to stand twice in the one spot to throw a shadow. He had a hell of a cough, and told us he'd been badly gassed in France. He was an expert at snaring possums and koalas, and had ridden a bike up from Victoria. He had brought with him a bundle of beautiful 'blue Monaro' brush-tail possum skins to put through the northern market. He struck me as one of those poor bastards that life has a snout on.

One night he told us he had married a Victorian girl when he came back from the war. He got a soldier settlement block later, and, being short of dough, he had gone possuming illegally to pay for the necessary improvements. He was caught, convicted and ended up losing the block. He told us miserably that his wife was with her mother in Melbourne, and added he hadn't seen her for six months.

Anyway, to get back to the possum snaring, Splinter took one side of the camp while Chilla and I worked the other. We went out with Splinter a couple of times, just to get the hang of it. There was a fair bit to learn. You had to pick the right tree to set your snares on, so Splinter showed us how to look for the claw marks in the trunk that showed it was a feed tree for possums. You then had to cut a sapling and lean it against the tree. This gave the possums a shortcut to climb up on. The piano wire then came into play. A thin wire noose was set about halfway up the sapling to snare the unfortunate animals. Koalas were a bit more difficult to catch – unlike possums, they camped in their feed trees. To catch them Splinter would put the wire noose on the end of a long pole and manually pull them out of the tree.

Chilla and I then started working our area. We concentrated on the brush-tails, Chilla wouldn't come at killing koalas. Snaring possums and koalas may seem a bit cruel, I suppose, but, after all, there were thousands of them about then, and a lot of people were starving.

Splinter was a great hand at living off the land. He would catch ducks by swimming underwater and pulling them down by the legs. He also seemed to be able to produce fish and yabbies at any time.

We used to go around our snares early each morning and skin our catch. We also had to reset our snares, sometimes moving the poles to another tree. We usually built a large fire and burnt the skinned possums. Back at camp we pegged the skins out to dry and had breakfast. Splinter sometimes threw a skinned possum on the coals. He said they were good eating, but they never made him put on any weight. He claimed the koalas were the best tucker. I tried the possums a few times, but never the koalas.

The Wonthaggi bloke was a happy-go-lucky sort who used to do quite well selling tie clips that he made. All he had was a piece of pine board with nails in it and tie wire. He could knock these little gadgets up in a couple of minutes.

'What the hell *were* these gadgets?' I asked him.

'Well, they saved you tying a knot in your tie every time you wore it. The tie was knotted onto this little wire frame that had a looped hook that slipped behind your collar.

Chilla reckoned it was a bloody great idea, not that he ever wore a tie.

'This bloke had a couple of ties to demonstrate the gadget. He sold a lot to shops, as well as in pubs. As I said, he came from Wonthaggi. I'd never heard of it before, but he used to sing a song about the place.'

Before I could stop him he burst into song.

*There's a part of my heart in Wonthaggi,*
*And it's calling me, calling me home.*

'That's all I remember of it, I'm afraid. Hey, whose shout is it?'

I heaved a silent prayer of thanks for his lapse of memory and told him it was his shout.

The publican wouldn't hear of it. He had brought Joan on duty and was concentrating on Snowy's yarn. 'No, my shout,' he said.

The dinner bell rang as the publican brought the beers over.

'Right, get it into you, Simmo, and we'll have a feed.'

We did that, leaving the publican without reward for his generosity.

At dinner Snowy had a glow up and told Maisie she was not only beautiful but the best waitress in the back country. She was embarrassed, but you could see she was tickled pink.

Next morning I saw Snowy's bed hadn't been slept in. I had a late breakfast to spare Maisie's feelings, then strolled along to the saddler's shop.

'Ah!' that worthy said as I walked in. 'The mail truck dropped those packs off.' And he jerked his thumb towards the back of the shop. I went through to a large room at the rear, where at least twenty packsaddles were thrown in an untidy heap that almost filled the room.

I returned to the front and asked the saddler if he wanted me to strip the flaps off out the back. He agreed that was the best place to do the job and handed me a trimming knife. The job of pulling the flaps off the pack-saddle trees took a couple of hours, then, by lunchtime, I had cut the linings off about half of them. It was a fairly slow job as I had to salvage the best of the straw bottle liners that formed the base of the lining.

By knock-off time I had all the flaps ready for relining, and carried them into the front workshop. The saddler inspected the heap of oaten liners, and said he'd see me the next day.

That night at dinner my mate seemed to be as happy as a wallaby in a wheatfield. It was a good meal, and afterwards we stretched out on our bunks.

Snowy patted his stomach. 'I'm putting on too much weight. A man should go for a jog. What do you think, Simmo?'

'Good idea,' I told him. 'Off you go, I'll wait for you here.'

'A nice sort of a bloody mate you are. I'd like to know your secret. I don't think they could fatten you if they fed you with a bloody shovel.'

I grinned at him and told him it was impossible to fatten thoroughbreds and mongrel dogs, then added, 'How about finishing that yarn?'

'Right you are, where was I up to?'

I told him, and, feeling his stomach again, he picked up where he had left off.

Well, every Saturday we hauled our skins up to the railway. We took turns pulling a small slide that Chilla had knocked up. Chilla and I usually had about eighty skins, and Splinter a few more. We caught a train to Moree, where there was a skin buyer. He paid us in cash, and I couldn't believe the money we were making. Splinter made straight for the post office, where he sent most of the money back to his wife.

The bloke from Wonthaggi always came to Moree with us. He went around the shops and the pubs, flogging the little gadgets he'd made during the week. Chilla and I did a bit of a pub crawl, then bought rations for the coming week.

We all had light swags with us, so met and camped just out of town. On Sunday morning we returned to our camp.

The only thing I didn't like about the possuming was that it was the breeding season. You couldn't avoid snaring females, and as a result the very young didn't survive. We kept a couple of older ones around the camp as pets. You wouldn't believe the bloody mischief a young possum can get up to, but rearing them made me feel a bit better about what we were doing.

The possum catch started to taper off after three weeks or so and we had to set our snares further away from the camp. Just the same, at the end of six weeks I felt like a billabong millionaire. Splinter was on top of the world and talking about being able to buy a small farm.

We went to Moree as usual that weekend. We did the usual rounds and then camped out of town. Splinter was very quiet, and that night he sat for a long time reading a letter he must have picked up at the post office. After some time he ripped it up and threw it in the fire.

Next day, back at the camp, we couldn't get a word out of him. About four o'clock in the afternoon he picked up his pliers and wire and walked off. We reckoned he was going to set a few extra traps. The rest of us took it easy.

By nightfall, when there was no sign of Splinter, we began to think he may have met with an accident. Chilla went out to the area he was working and cooeed for a while, but got no answer. When he came back, he said it was no use us blundering about in the dark trying to find him, it would be better to wait for daylight. We hoped he would turn up before then, but when dawn broke there was still no sight of our missing mate.

I expected Chilla to organise a search using the three of us to comb the bush. Instead, he picked up a waterbag, and, turning to us, told the bloke from Wonthaggi and me to wait in the camp until he returned. I protested, saying it would be quicker if we all went out. Chilla gave me a funny look.

'Snow,' he said, 'just do what I ask.'

Then he walked off in the direction Splinter had taken

the day before. He hadn't returned by four o'clock that afternoon, and I began to wonder what the hell was going on. The bloke from Wonthaggi reckoned a Yowie might have got them both, but I told him to keep his f...'n fairytales to himself. Shortly after, we heard the sound of a motor, and a utility truck appeared out of the timber. A young copper was driving, and I could see Chilla sitting beside him. There was no sign of Splinter.

Chilla got out and walked slowly over to us.

'I'm sorry, fellas, Splinter's dead.'

'Where is he, then?' I asked.

Chilla didn't say anything, just pointed to a tarp-covered shape on the back of the ute.

The young copper swaggered across from the vehicle. 'Yeah, the silly bastard hung himself with piano wire. If he'd been any heavier, it would have cut his frigging head off.'

Chilla rounded on him in a flash. 'Don't big-note yourself in front of these blokes. You were bloody useless back there, all you did was spew your guts out.'

The swagger went out of the copper like air from a pricked balloon. 'I've got to pick up his belongings,' he muttered.

Chilla jerked his thumb at Splinter's swag. 'Over there. Take them and get to hell out of here.'

The copper gathered our mate's few possessions. As he passed us, he tried to regain some authority. 'I'll need the three of you to come in to the station to make statements.'

Chilla gave him a cold look. 'If you want statements from us, you can come out in a car tomorrow morning and pick us up.'

I had made a fresh billy of tea. As the copper drove away, I poured out a mug and handed it to Chilla. He seemed calm enough, but I noticed that his hands shook that much he could hardly hold the mug.

We made the statements the cops wanted, and were the only ones at Splinter's funeral. I told the others I thought we should write to his widow, but Chilla said to leave it to the police.

'I'm sorry, fellas. Splinter's dead.'

The three of us stayed on until the end of July, when the possum season ended. It was never a very happy camp, though, after Splinter's death. But Chilla and I ended up clearing nearly fifty quid each out of the possuming, and that was a bloody fortune, I reckoned.

In Moree, the bloke from Wonthaggi left to go north to Queensland. Chilla and I were having a few beers, when he suddenly said, 'Snowy, my lad, I think it's time we visited the bright lights, and saw the seamier side of life.'

I asked him what the hell he was talking about.

'Sydney, Snowy, Sydney's the place. We can afford to lash out and have a holiday. It won't cost us that much, I know a cheap boarding house at Paddington we can stay at.'

Well, we booked into the pub we were drinking at and bought train tickets to the big smoke. Chilla and I each bought a new set of clobber, new boots and a suitcase.

I was standing outside one shop, waiting for Chilla, when I saw Joe, the rabble rouser, approaching. He propped when he saw me and snarled, 'You're the bastard who dobbed us into the coppers at Parkes.'

He swung a punch at me, but I grabbed his arm and, wheeling him around, pinned him up against the shop front. He was about fifty years old, and I held him there easily. I told him I didn't fight old men, and that it wasn't us who dobbed his crowd in.

'That's right, it was one of your own. Let him go, Snow.'

I turned my head to see Chilla standing behind me. I released Joe, and Chilla convinced him the police spy was in his own group. We walked up to a pub, and over a beer, he told us he only had the clothes on his back. He had lost everything else in a recent dust-up with the police and was broke. I couldn't help feeling sorry for the poor bastard. I hadn't forgotten what it was like to have bugger all.

As you know, it's a matter of honour to a bushman to shout in turn. I handed over a quid for the next round of drinks and, when no one was looking, slipped the change in front of him. The glance he gave me was thanks enough.

Anyway, Chilla and I left our swags at the pub and caught

the next mail train to Sydney. But you'll have to wait, Simmo, until some other time to hear about our spell in the big smoke. I'm going for a walk now to get rid of this spare tyre, I'll see you in the morning.

I said goodnight, and smiled to myself. I was sure Snowy had found a way to lose weight, but it had little to do with walking.

# 11

After breakfast next morning, I walked the half block to the saddler's shop. He greeted me cheerfully and handed me a large awl.

'Make yourself a six-strand wax end,' he said, and watched to see if I knew what he was talking about.

I put on the spare leather apron that was hanging on a nail, then found the hemp. Saddlers' hemp is always kept in a tin with a hole in the lid to prevent tangles. I knew he was watching me closely as I twisted off the strands in the approved manner.

Satisfied that I knew what I was doing, he went back to the job of replacing the seat in a stock saddle.

The saddler was probably in his sixties. He told me he had been a travelling saddler before he opened the shop, and had done the saddling on stations from the Gulf to Longreach. He was a cheerful character, with unruly grey hair and a round, ruddy face. When there were no visitors in the shop, he used to sing ditties. Although he knew I was there, he seemed to sing to amuse himself more than for my benefit. One, in particular, was a favourite of his. Each stanza started with a pronounced 'Oh!' It went like this:

> *Oh! I'm up to me knees in Mitchell grass,*
> *I'm up to me knees in clover,*
> *I'm up to the neck of me spurs in debt*
> *And I'm a flamin' drover.*

> *Oh! Budgereei and mind your eye*
> *And don't kick up a shindy,*
> *I've got a girl at Camooweal*
> *And another at Goondiwindi.*

> Oh! The Queensland track is a bugger of a track,
> There's never any grass or water,
> There I met an old pro on the Warrego
> Who asked me to marry her daughter.
>
>> Oh! budgereei and mind your eye
>> And don't kick up a shindy,
>> I've got a girl in Camooweal
>> And another in Goondiwindi.
>
> Oh! I took a job with a Top End mob,
> But the drover was a rotter,
> He would rant and roar so I broke his jaw
> And I left at Caradotta.
>
>> Oh! budgereei and mind your eye
>> And don't kick up a shindy,
>> I've got a girl in Camooweal
>> And another in Goondiwindi.

It took me two days to sew the pack linings on. I was in no hurry, as I thoroughly enjoyed the company of the singing saddler. I hadn't seen a great deal of Snowy during this time, but after finishing the packs I had a few drinks with him. That night he seemed in good spirits, so I reminded him he had once mentioned losing his virginity.

My mate thought for a minute or so. 'I don't remember that.'

'You don't remember losing your virginity?'

'No, I don't remember telling you about that.'

'You didn't, but I'd like to hear about it.'

'Fair enough – it happened in Sydney ...

After we finished the possuming, I told you Chilla and I hopped on the mail train to the big smoke. Riding on a train as a fare-paying passenger was a new experience for me, and I lapped it up, I can tell you. It was a real eye opener to me to see how the other half travelled. We were in second class, of course – but the first class carriages were fully booked. It seemed that despite the depression some people were still well off.

The train pulled in to Central Station, and I couldn't help remembering the last time I was there. I walked past the toilet I had hidden in, then stopped and had a leak there for old times' sake.

Outside the station Chilla hailed a cab and gave the driver directions. Right from the start, old Chilla looked just as much at home in the city as in the bush. The taxi driver dropped us off at a boarding house in Paddington, and we booked in at the reception desk and headed up to our room on the second floor. At the bottom of the stairs we stood aside to let a woman pass. She was built like a brick toilet and wore more jewellery than you could poke a stick at.

'Why, if it's not Mr O'Rourke,' she cried. 'It must be four years since we've seen you.'

Chilla took off his hat. 'Hello, Mrs Flannery. It's good to be back in town.'

Chilla introduced me, and told her we'd be staying for a fortnight. After chatting for a few minutes, we went up to the room and unpacked our few possessions.

'Right,' said Chilla. 'When in Rome, do as the Romans do. Let's go and buy some city clobber and get out of these moleskins.'

We bought a couple of sets of town clobber and a new hat each. The brims were three and a quarter inches and would do in both city and the bush. I got a pair of town shoes, but Chilla bought a pair of riding boots. He said they might come in handy and they were quite smart. Just the same, I wondered about those riding boots, and I realised just how little I knew about my mate. I knew from experience that he could fight and shear, but despite knocking around with him for eighteen months, all I knew about his past was that he had gone to the war. I had asked him a couple of times where he came from, but he always dodged the question; having told him my life story, I felt a bit cheated. I thought then that old Chilla liked to pass himself off as a man of mystery, and I reckoned that was a flaw in his character. Mind you, I never told him that.

Anyway, we had a great time in Sydney. We went to shows and to the pictures, we drank at various pubs and, overall, lived the life of Riley. There were a lot of smaller halls in the city where people gathered for community singing. It was cheap entertainment, where the hard-up could forget their troubles for a while at least.

Mrs Flannery fussed around Chilla like an old mother hen. She had our washing and ironing done for us, and told me any friend of Chilla's was always welcome under her roof.

On the surface, Sydney seemed prosperous enough. Behind the scenes, though, I reckoned the depression had hit the city as hard, if not harder, than in the bush. There were soup kitchens for the down-and-outs, and there was real misery in parts of the city. Unlike out west, the blokes on the dole didn't have to move on to get the next ration coupons. As a result, there were ghetto-like areas in the city where the unemployed existed in absolute poverty. One day Chilla and I went to one of these places, called Happy Valley. He was looking for an old mate of his. He didn't find him, but to be there with a quid in my pocket made me feel bloody guilty. The only happy thing about that valley was its name.

Being in Sydney, it was easy to keep up with what was happening. The papers were full of the activities of a group called the New Guard. They were a radical mob started by ex-army officers. It seemed to me they were against commos, Jews and, above all, Lang. Chilla reckoned they were more right wing than Genghis Khan. You had to be a bit careful at times, as there were some lively brawls between these New Guard blokes and traditional Labor supporters. It was one of these New Guards who later cut the ribbon at the opening of the Harbour Bridge. The arch of the bridge was joined up when we were in Sydney – the bloody thing did look like a coathanger then.

We had been in Sydney for about ten days, when one

evening Chilla told me it was time for my initiation into manhood. He took me to this house of ill fame in Paddington where the madame greeted him like an old friend. 'I want you to break in this mate of mine,' he told her, and before I knew it I was in a room with this sheila. Well, I won't go into details, but it was an experience, I can tell you. I reckoned, though, I was too confused and embarrassed to get full value, so, without telling Chilla, I went back the next night and saddled up again.

The experience was a revelation to me. I suppose I was pretty innocent, but those days there wasn't much to stir the passions. The closest thing to pornography was advertisements for women's corsets. Up till then I'd never regarded any of the women I'd met as sex objects, but after that second night, I found myself mentally undressing every female I met. It worried me a bit, I thought I was turning into a serial rapist, but once I got back to the bush I forgot all that nonsense.

At the end of the fortnight we farewelled Mrs Flannery and caught a cab to the station. The spell in the big smoke had cost a bit, but I still had enough left to give me a healthy reserve fund.

It was late in the day when the train pulled into Moree, so we decided to let our heads go and camp at the pub. The place was busy, as there were a number of drovers there who had brought mobs in from Queensland. Moree was a major trucking centre those days. Chilla looked the drovers over with interest. They were always big spenders at the end of a long trip, and I knew Chilla's mind was devising some method of extracting a quid or two from them.

Chilla showed his hand in the bar after dinner. He bought a couple of the men a drink and mentioned casually that there would be a game of poker on in our room a bit later. He then bought a bottle of rum and we went upstairs. Chilla put one of the suitcases on the floor and threw a towel over it. He sat down on the floor with his legs crossed, then shuffled the cards and dealt us both a hand. He grinned at me.

'We'll have a hand or two while we wait to see who takes the bait.'

We didn't have long to wait. There was a thumping of boots on the stairs and four blokes crowded into the room. They were typical Queensland cattlemen, as tough as the life they lived. They had obviously all lashed out and bought new riding boots and clobber, but not hats. As you know, Simmo, stockmen will wear their hats night and day until they bloody well fall to pieces.

I reckon you can tell a lot about a man by the bash he puts in his hat and the way he wears it. Anyway, they all had a rum and squatted on the floor. I had no wish to chance losing my money, so I lay down on my bed and watched the game.

Chilla shuffled the cards and gave them to a drover to cut. The blind was set at two bob, and the game started. I watched for a while; Chilla only won one pot before I went to sleep. I wondered if he was foxing, or if his luck had deserted him. I remember hearing our visitors leaving in the small hours, then I went back to sleep.

At breakfast next morning, I asked Chilla about the game. He told me the drovers were no mugs at poker. There had been no big losers, but, he added casually, he had finished up three quid in front. As we smoked after the meal, Chilla said the poker players had invited him down to their camp for a game of two-up in the afternoon. 'Snowy,' he said, 'as the Gods are smiling on us, we'll sleep in sheets again tonight.'

A little after four o'clock we wandered down to where the drovers were camped. Chilla's eyes lit up when he saw there were two droving teams in the one camp. With practised ease he took control and ran the game himself. Chilla always used three pennies. He liked quick results, and as the ring master was paid by the winners, he kept raking in the dough.

The game continued until almost dark. There was a top camp cook among the group, so we stayed for a feed of corned beef and camp oven bread. After the meal the rum bottle went the rounds and the yarns started. I listened open mouthed to the tales of rushes and dry stages. One day, I promised myself, I'd head for Queensland and experience it all myself.

The drovers planned to start back north the next day, so after a few more rums we wished them luck and made our way back to the pub. After breakfast next morning, we had a council of war. It would probably be more accurate to say Chilla outlined our future plans. We had done well out of possums, he said, now we would try our hand with rabbits and pigs.

Wild pigs had raided our possum snaring camp a few times, and had become a real problem in the bush. We heard that the Moree pasture protection board were paying sixpence for each pig snout. Now that doesn't seem much, but for a zack you could buy a pound of beef. Rabbit skins were worth two bob a pound, and you could get at least a zack for the whole bunny. We were in a fortunate position. We had money up our sleeves, and could afford to try our luck. In Sydney, I had been surprised to find that the city people depended as much on the rabbit for meat as we did in the bush. Chilla often said that without goats and rabbits, no family could have survived in the bush.

We packed up our good clobber and left the suitcases with the publican. Chilla still had his old .22 rifle, so he bought two packets of long rifle ammunition, and after some mental arithmetic, he paid for a dozen rabbit traps as well. We purchased rations for a couple of weeks, including two pounds of dried apricots. The apricots had me a bit puzzled for a while – I'd never seen Chilla eat pudding of any kind.

There weren't many rabbits around the town itself. Apparently the little blighters didn't like the soil there. Further up the Gwydir, though, past where we had been possuming, both rabbits and pigs were supposed to be in plague numbers. Chilla made a few phone calls and got permission to operate on a property up near Gravesend. Chilla said we would catch the next day's train out to Gravesend, so we went out to our old town camp for the night.

On the way out of town we passed the town dump. Chilla

rummaged around and came away with a broken-down pram, two empty kerosene tins and some nails. He threw the lot on the slide, and we headed on out. As soon as we got to the camp, Chilla started on our transport. He got an axle and pair of wheels off the pram and fixed them to the bottom of the slide, using nails and tin strips off the lid of a kero tin. He stood back and looked the contraption over.

'There you are,' he grinned, 'we've now got a bloody rickshaw. All we need is a coolie to pull it.'

Next morning we rolled up to the station and bought tickets to Gravesend. The rickshaw caused a bit of comment, but people were becoming used to unemployed blokes using odd ways of carting their gear about.

There wasn't a lot to see at Gravesend – a store, a pub, a one-man police station and a few houses. Chilla and I wasted no time heading out to the run where we were going to set up camp. The wheels were a great idea. We could walk at full pace, with the rickshaw following like a dog. We camped not far from a billabong that was full of pig wallows, and, unlike Moree, the softer soil there had plenty of rabbit warrens.

As soon as we had set up the camp, Chilla got the old .22 rifle out of his swag and screwed the stock to the block and barrel. He cleaned and oiled the old relic, and then checked the sights by firing half a dozen shots into a tin nailed to a tree. It was obvious that Chilla was a crack shot.

We had a drink of tea, then Chilla topped the billy up and stuck it back to boil again. As soon as it bubbled, he tossed another half handful of tea leaves in. I wondered how he was going to drink that brew, but Chilla had other ideas, and the mystery of the apricots was soon revealed. He got two dozen out of the bag and, with his pocketknife, he made two small holes in each one. When the tea had cooled a bit, he tipped it into the bottom of one of the kero tins and threw the apricots in. The cunning old bastard had just made ten bobs' worth of pig snouts.

Despite Chilla's skill with the old .22, we soon found that it didn't have enough punch to knock over a full-grown pig.

At the end of the first week, we only had two dozen snouts, most of them from small pigs. We had better luck with the rabbits. There were huge warrens everywhere, and we seldom found an empty trap. We made bows to dry the skins on from plain wire that Chilla had knocked off from the boundary fence.

I pulled him up. 'What were these bows?'

Well, you took about three feet of wire, then you'd bend it into a bow and push both ends into the ground. The skin is stretched over it and held in place by knotting the hind legs.

Anyway, we did all right with the bunnies – they made us a quid and kept us in meat. On our first trip into Moree, we sold ten pound of skins. Chilla had decided not to cash in the pig snouts at that point. He had dried the apricots and mixed them with the snouts, and to tell you the truth it was hard to tell the bloody difference, but Chilla reckoned we'd leave them until the whole lot had become riper. That way, a close examination was unlikely.

We had a few beers at the pub we'd stayed at, and Chilla talked the publican into lending him a .303 rifle. We bought rations and a box of .303 cartridges, then had a late session at the pub. On the way out of town to camp, we passed a hall where a dance was in progress. I'd never seen a dance before, and I was fascinated. We stood at the door for a while, listening to the music and watching the dancers. Later, in camp, Chilla asked me if I liked dancing. I told him I'd never seen a dance before. 'Well,' he said, 'you should learn.'

When we got back to our main camp, Chilla tried the .303 out – and from that point on, the pigs went down like nine pins. We got so many that Chilla thought it was safe to doctor up a few more apricots. We shifted camp a few times, but one thing we didn't have to do was dispose of the pigs' carcasses. The bloody pigs did that for us. They didn't mind dining on their own kind. That's the reason I still won't eat pork to this day.

Chilla waited until he had a bag of a hundred snouts and

apricots before he went to the office of the pasture protection board with them. They hunted him out of the office and told him to go around the back, where they would be dealt with. A bloke came out and gave them a rough count. And it was bloody rough, I can tell you – he tipped them out and raked them around with a stick while he held his nose.

Both the pigs and the rabbits were now bringing in good money, not as much as the possums, but a lot better than wages. One night after we'd been out about three weeks, Chilla built up a big fire and raked clear a large area out from it.

'Right, young Snowy,' he said, 'you like dancing. Get over here and I'll teach you how.'

He did, too. Thank God we were out in the scrub. Anyone seeing us would have thought we were off our flaming heads. Anyway, by following behind him and copying his movements, I learnt to waltz, and then to do the quick step. Chilla reckoned once you had mastered those two, the rest was easy – all you had to do was follow the couple in front of you. Each night, Chilla would sit by the fire and whistle while I danced. I felt a real bloody idiot, but Chilla was a hard bloke to say no to.

The next time we caught the train to Moree, we stayed at the pub. We got our suitcases, had a clean up and put on the gear we'd bought in Sydney. We had a drink before the evening meal. I was well under drinking age, but looked a lot older than my years, so was never challenged. About eight o'clock Chilla suggested we go for a walk, and, as if by accident, we found ourselves at the dance hall. I suspected Chilla had planned the whole thing. He paid for us both at the door and led the way into the hall. There was a complicated sort of dance in progress, which I learnt later was a Pride of Erin. Chilla left me standing near the door and next minute he was on the floor with a good-looking girl.

He came back at the end of the dance. 'That's all there is to it, Snow. Now the next one is an old time waltz, you can do that. Wait until there are a few couples dancing, then come over with me. You know what to say. The sooner you start the easier it will be.'

Well, my knees were knocking, I reckon, but I walked over with Chilla. He asked a girl to dance, and I muttered something to the girl sitting on the next seat. Anyway, she got up, and somehow I managed to get through until the music stopped. I found I was concentrating so hard on the dance steps that I forgot I had a girl in my arms. That finally got rid of any lingering fears I had of becoming a sex maniac.

The next dance was a gipsy tap. I watched for a couple of minutes, then decided it was no more than a bit of waltzing and a slide. The girl I had danced with before was still sitting down, so I slid over, and this time I got the words out properly. We talked a little during the dance, and she laughed when I nearly slid out of the door with her.

After the dance finished, she said she'd like a drink, so I bought us both a lemonade at the drinks booth. She asked me where I came from and, after a second's thought, I told her I was from Sydney. That seemed to impress her. I've always found that girls from country towns are keen on getting to know strangers. I suppose I looked the part, too, in city clobber, with my hair slicked down with brilliantine – and, after all, I was a good-looking young fellow, those days.

My dance partner took a ladylike sip of lemonade and asked me where I was working now. I dare say she expected me to say at a bank, or at least with a stock and station agent. I suppose I could have pulled the wool over her eyes, but I remembered that honesty is the best policy and told her I was camped on the river, shooting pigs. She burst into a fit of the giggles.

'Here I am,' she said, 'acting like lady muck, and you're a pig shooter.' Seeing that I was embarrassed, she stopped laughing. 'Don't worry, I'm glad you're not a Sydney toff. My dad's a fettler on the railway.'

The next dance was what they called the black bottom. It was one of those crazy dances popular in the twenties, I believe. Anyway, we sat it out and yarned. I saw Chilla nodding approval from the front door. We had a few more dances that night, and from then on there was no stopping me, I went to every Saturday night dance until we left Moree.

Chilla was pleased with my progress. No doubt, he felt my education was going well. After getting off the train at Gravesend one day, we bought a few things at the store and ended up in a session at the pub. It was owned by a foreign couple. I think they owned the store as well. Someone said they were Lebanese, but Chilla just called them camel drivers. Anyway, in our group at the pub were a couple of other rabbit trappers, a couple of stockmen, a big bloke who said he was a shearer and a character called 'the Judge'. The Judge was a well known storyteller, who never let the truth get in the way of a good yarn. Most people took his stories with a grain of salt, which was just as well, for most of them were a bit hard to swallow. We learnt that the Judge got his nickname from his place of work. He was employed at the railway goods shed at Gravesend, and could be found there at any time sitting on a case. It didn't matter if it was a fruit case or a kerosene case – the Judge deliberated on them all.

The talk got around to possuming. It was then illegal, but was still going on. There were reports that the police were using undercover cops to try and stamp out the practice. The Judge scoffed at the idea.

'Rubbish,' he said, 'those undercover cops couldn't find their backside in two grabs. Last weekend I went out and caught ten of the best possums you ever saw, the fur on the little bastards was as long as your index finger.'

The big bloke who said he was a shearer pulled a badge out of his shirt pocket. 'Is that a fact?' he said. 'Well, I happen to be a policeman.'

The Judge never blinked an eye. 'Is that a fact?' he replied. 'Well, I happen to be the biggest liar in New South Wales.'

The bar room exploded in laughter, and the copper, having blown his cover for no good reason, departed.

We packed up and went in to Moree for Christmas. We had found a boarding house that was a lot cheaper than staying at the pub. It was not a happy time. Scullin had been defeated by Joe Lyons, leading the United Australia Party.

By that time I had more money than I knew what to do with. I didn't feel comfortable carrying a roll of notes around with me, so I opened an account with the Commonwealth Savings Bank at the Moree Post Office. Chilla hated banks, but in the end he opened an account, too. 'If you can't beat the bastards, I suppose you might as well join them,' he growled.

We had done well snaring and shooting around Moree, but it wasn't in Chilla's nature to stay in one place for ever. He decided we should try our luck further west. We left our good clobber at the boarding house, returned the .303 to the publican, then, after saying our goodbyes, we jumped a train to Narrabri. There was no need for us to jump the rattler, as we both had plenty of moolah. But Chilla believed in the saying, waste not want not. He called it travelling economy class. He reckoned we had to break the bad habit of paying our fare on the Gravesend line.

We caught a goods train travelling south at about nine o'clock that night. The engine was pulling a number of goods wagons. They weren't locked, those days, just fastened from the outside. Chilla found one that wasn't quite full – he checked the chalk mark on the wagon, then, satisfied, he opened it fully and we crawled in. Chilla pulled the sliding door almost shut, jamming it there with a piece of coal. I thought it was to let a bit of air in, but Chilla informed me of the real reason.

'Snow, my lad,' he said, 'we want to leave this wagon just before Narrabri. If that door becomes locked, we could end up God knows where.'

Anyway, we did leave the wagon – at a little place called Edgar, or a name like that. I remember it because it started me thinking of the bloke we had camped with at Parkes. It was still dark, so we waited for daylight, then walked about eight miles to a creek, where we camped for the day. The following day we humped our swags down the creek to where it joined the Namoi River. A few days later we were in Wee Waa, and a couple of weeks later we got to Walgett.

We set up camp on the river and had a bludge for a couple of days. Then Chilla came back to the camp one day with the news that there was to be an auction on later that afternoon. The horses, saddles and packs of a deceased drover were to go up for sale. Chilla rolled a smoke and lit it. 'Snowy, my boy,' he said, 'the time has come to give foot slogging away. We will saddle up and head for the sunset.'

Well, we went to the auction, and Chilla waited for a while to see what the horses brought. Bidding was slow, and after half a dozen had gone cheaply, he slipped in and bought two good-looking saddle horses and a couple of packhorses. The top price he paid was five bob. Once the horses were sold, the auctioneer started on the gear. There was not a lot of interest. Again Chilla waited, ignoring the pointed looks from the man with the hammer. Finally he had two riding saddles and bridles as well as two packs knocked down to him. All as cheap as dirt, Chilla reckoned. The gear certainly looked to be in good condition; a bit of grease was all it needed. We had put a couple of quid each into the venture. Chilla paid in cash, and put the horses in a small separate yard. I helped him carry the saddles and packs a little way out from the yards and looked over our new possessions with interest.

'Well, Snowy,' Chilla said, opening a packbag. 'We've scored hobbles, bells and a halter or two here – we've just about got all we want. We'll camp here tonight, and try the nags out in the morning.'

Chilla went up town and arrived back with our swags and gear in a taxi. He also had some rations and leather dressing. I went over to the yard and looked at our horses. The world was going to the dogs, and here I was proud part owner of four fine-looking steeds.

Next morning we saddled up the riding horses – and one of those fine-looking steeds threw me as high as a country toilet. I got no sympathy from Chilla. He just laughed, caught the mare and got on it himself. You know, the bloody thing just walked away with him like a lady's hack. She was a pretty bay mare I called Music. Afterwards Chilla showed me the correct way to get on a horse. He made me practise jamming my left knee into the horse's shoulder and using that as a pivot. From then on, I had no trouble with the mare. Chilla had picked a big grey stockhorse. To keep the musical theme going, he christened him Minstrel.

Old Chilla never ceased to amaze me. At one stage of his chequered career he must have had a bit to do with horses. Once we got the nags and gear organised, we shifted camp down to the river. The weather was still too hot to do much, but when we were offered the chance to do some roo shooting, we were more than pleased. As you know, there's nothing worse than sitting around in a camp. We threw the packs on and rode out to this company station where the roos were as thick as grasshoppers.

Chilla talked the manager into lending us some ex-army rifles and ammo, then, with the packs loaded with station beef, we set up camp at a bore about forty miles out. The roos really were in plague proportions. The wet hadn't arrived and, with water scarce, the marsupials had to depend on the station waters. There has been a lot of rubbish written about killing roos. You and I both know that the kangaroo population has hit the roof since station waters were established. Anyway, we did quite well out of the roo skins, and stayed there shooting until it rained. There had been heavy falls up in Queensland, and we heard that the Macintyre and the Moonie were in full flood. Chilla reckoned we had better try and make it over the Barwon before the northern waters came down.

Rain was falling, and the Barwon was in flood, when we got there. Chilla looked at the river and pushed his hat back. 'Snowy, my lad,' he said, 'it will be dark in an hour, but we'll have to cross this evening, before the Macintyre water gets here. First, I'll see what these nags are like in water.'

We rode downstream until Chilla selected a crossing place. He then pulled the saddle off Minstrel, and told me to unsaddle my mare, then, leading Music, he rode into the flood bareback. The current caught them, but both horses swam well and Chilla finally turned them around and returned to the bank. He and the horses came out quite a distance from their starting point. I was bloody pleased to see them back on solid ground, I can tell you. The thought had crossed my mind that I'd be in a nice mess if Chilla had been drowned.

We gave the horses a spell for a little while, then saddled up again. Chilla told me to cross my stirrups over the saddle, in case my mare got a hind hoof caught in an iron. We then stripped off and tied our clothes to the pummel of the saddles. I had never swum a river on horseback before, but Chilla told me not to worry. He said that he would take the lead, and all I had to do was put the packhorses into the river behind him.

Once we got out a little, the current hit us, and we seemed to be going downstream without getting closer to the far bank. Chilla kept looking back and nodding encouragement.

About halfway over, one of the packhorses started rearing and plunging. I urged my mare over towards him, but Chilla shouted to me to keep out of the way. The packhorse, after struggling in panic, disappeared under the surging floodwater. Our horses finally fought their way up the Walgett side of the Barwon, and stood there with heaving flanks. Chilla didn't seem too worried about the lost packhorse and gear, but it was my swag that had gone downstream with the water-logged bastard.

We had crossed the river about ten miles below the town. The ground was heavy, the horses were weary and it was almost dusk. Chilla decided we would camp back on a timbered ridge out from the Barwon and go into Walgett the next morning.

Well, we put in a miserable night on that bloody ridge. We did get a good fire going, but the only cover we had was a small tarp we'd bought from the station, and I was without a swag. I was bloody pleased to see daylight, I can tell you. The fire had gone out, and we had a dingo's breakfast – you know, a drink of water and a look around. The Barwon had risen overnight. The water from up north had come down and floodwater was roaring past, carrying uprooted trees with it.

Anyway, we packed up and rode through pouring rain into Walgett. We picked a dry camp by the trucking yards and unpacked. We put the horses in a yard, and when Chilla suggested we head up town for a hot meal, he got no argument from me. We were both soaked to the skin and bloody hungry. Before eating ourselves, we called at one of the agents and arranged for hay to be taken down to the yards for the horses.

Later we bought dry clothes, a decent tarpaulin and replenished our rations. The taxi driver who took us to the camp told us that Albert Jacka had died in poverty during the previous month. He said that after failing in business, Jacka had taken a job selling soap. Chilla reckoned it was a bloody disgrace that Australia's first VC should finish up like that.

It rained for a bloody week, and Chilla's mood reflected the weather. I was pleased to see the sun finally break through and the ground dry out. In the pub one day we got talking to a smart-looking chap. He said he was originally from Victoria and had knocked about a bit down there. He had been digging spuds by hand for seven pence a bag, when he decided to try his luck further north. He went on to say he had reached Lightning Ridge the year before. He reckoned he'd had new chum's luck, for out at the three mile he had picked up a parcel of opal worth two hundred pounds. He told us he'd been a bloody fool and had blown the lot in Sydney. Chilla looked at him. I could see my mate was expecting the opal gouger to put the fangs in.

Chilla wasn't wrong. The bloke said he still had the claim and was sure there was a second level. His problem was, he admitted, he was broke and couldn't afford to get to the Ridge to work the claim.

This bloke didn't actually ask us for money – having baited the hook, he changed the subject, and finally left us saying he hoped to run into us again. That night Chilla and I talked about the opal gouger and his supposed rich claim.

'You know, Snowy,' Chilla said, 'I've always thought I'd like to have a go at digging opals. What do you think?'

It wasn't like Chilla to fall for a con man – but I told him I'd leave it up to him.

'Fair enough, Snow, but we'll have to check out this character before we commit ourselves. If he's fair dinkum, the experience will be worth it.'

In the end we decided he was all talk. But that, Simmo, is – as the lift driver said to the lady – another story.'

Snowy loved to toss in a simile whenever the opportunity arose. I wasn't impressed by his last effort, but said goodnight without comment.

## 12

I didn't see much of Snowy the following day. I spent most of the time at the saddlers – he had a couple of small jobs he wanted me to do. He was an entertaining sort of chap and I enjoyed his company. He insisted on shouting me lunch, so it was not until late afternoon that I saw Snowy. I found him in the bar drinking with two young fencers. I joined them and learnt from the pair that they were heading south at daylight the next morning. On the way to the kitchen I noticed their vehicle parked in the backyard.

Over dinner it was obvious to me that there was a lot of tension between my mate and Maisie. It was none of my business, so I didn't interfere. I decided to have an early night, and went over to Snowy's room and stretched out on my bunk. Snowy appeared an hour or so later. He flung himself down on his bed. 'Bloody women,' he growled, then lapsed into brooding silence.

I knew the only way to cheer Snowy up was to get him to talk. I lay there thinking about the best way to start him off, then asked, 'Did you end up going to Lightning Ridge with that opal man, Snowy?'

My mate said nothing for a few minutes, then responded as I hoped he would ...

No, Simmo, we didn't. We stayed in our camp at the trucking yards for a while after it fined up. Chilla and I went up town fairly regularly and often saw him. He would always say hello and look at us expectantly, but Chilla just nodded. After this went on a few times, I asked Chilla if we were going to join him in the opal mining venture.

Chilla looked at me. 'I thought you would have worked him out by now, Snow. He's a con man.'

I realised then that Chilla had been waiting for me to

declare the opal gouger a fraud. I told him that I'd had my suspicions of the man, but wasn't sure. He sighed and shook his head. 'Snowy, you must learn to use your eyes. Have you ever seen a man who has used a pick and shovel who has hands that are as soft as a woman's?'

I had to admit I hadn't noticed.

'Well, Snowy, he's a con man, and a good one. Remember, he's never actually asked us for money, and only the experts can get people to give them dough without putting the fangs in.'

About a week after the rain cleared, we saw the common ranger riding up to our camp. He was a wiry little bloke with a large moustache. Reining up, he threw one leg over the pommel of the saddle and spoke. 'G'day, did you blokes lose a packhorse in the Barwon a few weeks ago?'

We told him we had, and waited for him to continue.

'Well, a horse and pack were found hung up in a tree about fifteen miles down the river. The pack and a swag that was on it are up at the police station.'

I looked at him with a bit of interest and said it must have been a messy job getting the gear off the horse. He gave me a bored sort of look.

'Son, it wasn't the first dead horse I've seen – I was with the artillery in France.' With that, he found his off-iron again and rode off.

Chilla and I went up and got the pack and other gear. Once we had greased the pack and bags, they looked none the worse for their trip down the Barwon. I had got myself another swag and clothes, but was keen to see if the oilskin wallet in my swag had survived the dipping. In it I had an old notebook and a number of clippings from papers. To my relief, I found I could separate the clippings, and laid them out to dry properly. The notebook was intact. Had the writing been in ink, it would probably have been ruined, but being in pencil, it was just a bit faded.

We had our horses hobbled out on the common on good feed not far from the yards. Running with them was a good sort of clumper with fairly clean legs. As we needed another packhorse, Chilla made inquiries about the gelding and found it was owned by our mate the common ranger. He advised Chilla that the gelding was four years old and unbroken. After some haggling, Chilla paid him ten bob for the horse, and got permission to use the yards to break it in.

We had the unbroken gelding in the round yard and were looking it over, when a young jackaroo wandered up to the yards and joined us. He was working on the property we had been shooting roos on, and we had met him a couple of times before. We yarned for a while, and it was no surprise to me to find the young bloke telling Chilla his life story. Chilla was like that, people seemed to trust him and were prepared to take him into their confidence. The talk was mostly idle for a while, then I pricked up my ears.

'Yes,' the young chap was saying, 'I've been given this great offer. I've got a bit of money together that I was going to send to my mother in Newcastle, but I've got the chance to double it in no time by investing in opal.'

'That's interesting,' said Chilla. 'How did you get on to that?'

'Well, I met this chap who has a very rich opal mine at Lightning Ridge. If I give him the money, he'll cut me in as a sleeping partner. I'll get half the profits and still be able to keep my job here.'

Chilla thought for a little while, then asked him when the deal was going to be finalised.

'Well, I've got to go back to the station tomorrow and get a cheque from the bookkeeper, then I'll come back on the weekend and fix things up.'

Chilla seemed satisfied with that information. Then just before the jackaroo left, Chilla asked him if he knew when the next train left for the coast. The young bloke said there was a mixed train leaving that night at eight. He had come into town with the manager, he said, to drop parcels off at the goods shed.

We wished the jackaroo luck and said we might see him on the weekend. After he had gone, Chilla decided to leave working on the gelding until the next day. We turned him out with our other horses and returned to our camp. Chilla was whistling quietly to himself as he put the billy on, and I knew from past experience that he was working on some sort of devious plan.

At six o'clock Chilla said he thought a stroll up town was in order. We called at the nearest pub and had a few drinks, then we went to the next pub and had another two rounds. We were drinking our second drink, when in walked the opal man. Chilla called him over and shouted him a beer. As he finished the drink, Chilla turned and faced him.

'We've got a bit of unfinished business,' Chilla said. 'I've got something to give you ... but this is no place to talk business – let's find somewhere a bit more private.'

The con man's face lit up in anticipation. 'Good idea, where did you have in mind?'

'Well, let's just go for a walk,' Chilla answered.

We left the pub and walked down the street. The lighting was very poor and when we came to a vacant allotment Chilla paused.

'This will do nicely,' said Chilla, and walked well into the block. We followed him and caught up once he'd stopped. Chilla faced the con man and in a casual voice said, 'Now I've got something for you.'

'Good, I can give you a receipt, if you wish.'

'Don't bother,' said my mate, and punched him in the guts.

The con man doubled up and gasped. 'W-what d-did you ...'

Chilla hauled him up by the collar. 'You've jumped my claim. As an opal miner, you should know what happens to claim jumpers. This is my territory – if anyone is going to be conned here, I'll do it.'

The con man tried hard to create a picture of wounded innocence. 'You could have just told me,' he muttered.

'I could have,' Chilla said. 'And now I *am* going to tell you something. You are going back to wherever you're staying, you're going to pack your gear and you're going to catch the eight o'clock train out of here. Do you understand?'

The con man nodded, but his eyes were giving another message.

'If you don't,' Chilla told him, 'I'll break every bone in your miserable body. But just to make sure you do, we're going to escort you to the station.'

At ten to eight the three of us walked onto the station platform. The sergeant of police, who we had met when picking up the pack, strolled over to us. 'Are you chaps leaving town?' he asked.

'No, sergeant, just our mate here,' said Chilla, indicating the con man. 'He's leaving for the coast for health reasons.'

The following day we ran our horses in and put the unbroken gelding in the small round yard. Chilla had borrowed a greenhide rope from the common ranger – he said that was all he needed to break in the new horse. He caught Minstrel and, tying the reins around the grey's neck, he put him in with the gelding. He left the two together for half an hour, then quietly entered the yard and, untying the grey's reins, slipped onto him bareback. Keeping the unbroken horse between Minstrel and the yard rails, Chilla began the first steps in breaking in the colt. He ran his hands over the youngster from the rump to his ears, doing this from both sides of the colt. Then after half an hour, he asked me to give him the halter and rope. Chilla repeated the handling process using the halter instead of his hands, and within a few minutes he had the halter on the gelding. He did up both the throat strap and chin strap, slipping the ring in the rope onto the latter.

After taking Minstrel out of the yards, he let the young horse out into a bigger yard and began lunging him. Chilla told me this was one of the most important lessons for a young horse, and we both know this is true. Stockhorses have to be caught in the open, so they have to be taught to face you. Lunging a stockhorse is far different to what dressage people call lunging. The youngster has to be constantly and

'No, Sergeant, just our mate here,' said Chilla, indicating the con man. 'He's leaving for the coast for health reasons.'

forcibly pulled around to face you, getting a pat and a soft word when he starts to respond.

The next lesson, Chilla said, was to teach the youngster to tie up. We had previously filled up a corn sack with wet soil and snigged it over to the yards. The rails of the yard were about six feet high. Chilla passed the greenhide rope over a stout top rail, then secured it to the sack. He then tied the end of the rope that remained to the bottom of the yard post so that the young horse could not pull the sack over the rail. He explained that if and when the horse moved forward, the weight would come off his neck and, that way, he would not only learn to tie up, but would also receive the first lesson in leading. Chilla told me the reason for everything he did, and I knew he was educating me as well as the young horse. It was obvious to me that Chilla knew a lot about horses, and I put it down to him having been in the Light Horse.

We went and had smoko by the yards and watched the young horse. The other packhorse's name was Digger, so Chilla reckoned we'd call the gelding Gunner. When I asked him why, he grinned.

'Well, we'll ride and pack this bloke, so he's gunner do both jobs – he's also a typical light artillery horse.'

We watched Gunner fight the rope for some time, until finally he woke up that it was better to move forward. He kept pulling away again, however, and the process had to be repeated. After a lengthy smoke, we went over and Chilla untied the rope. He climbed into the yard and again lunged the colt. After rewarding Gunner by fussing over him, Chilla walked to the side and made the horse walk around to face him. He did this for some time, flicking him on the rump with the end of the rope if he held back. After a little while he stood in front of Gunner and pulled the rope forward. With a bit of gentle urging, the youngster took a few tentative steps toward him. Chilla seemed satisfied with that, and after spending some time rubbing Gunner's neck and shoulders, he called out to me to bring in a pair of hobbles.

'Now, Snowy, I'm going to bag the horse down, and I want

you to hold his head. Remember, get a tight grip of the rope close to his head, and always stand on the side of the horse that I'm working on.'

I held Gunner as Chilla picked up both the colt's front feet and then put the hobbles on. Chilla then took the rope from me and pulled Gunner around. The colt struggled with the hobbles and almost fell over. Chilla explained he'd done that so the young horse would know he was restricted before the bagging started. As I held Gunner, Chilla rubbed him over with the bag and progressed to almost flogging him with it. After a while Gunner took little notice of what was going on. All the time, Chilla was talking to the horse in a quiet, monotonous voice. After he stopped, I almost laughed, as Gunner turned his head and looked at my mate as if to say, what the hell are you going to do to me next?

Chilla proceeded to pick up the colt's hind feet, standing close in to his flank as he did so. He explained that a horse could not hurt you if you stood there. If he cow kicked, he could do no more than push you away. Satisfied with his work on Gunner's hindquarters, Chilla stood back and looked the colt over.

'Right, Snow, we'll tidy up his mane and tail.'

Pulling out his pocketknife, Chilla went to work on the knots and tangles in Gunner's tail. By the time he had finished work on Gunner's mane, our new horse looked pretty smart, and Chilla decided it was time to boil the billy for lunch. We tied Gunner up to the bag again and retired to our temporary camp by the yard. I swallowed a mouthful of corned beef and looked at my mate. I knew he didn't like talking about his past, but I thought, to hell with it, and asked him if he had learnt horse breaking in the Light Horse.

He gave me one of his guarded looks. 'No, Snowy, I was never in the Light Horse.' He stopped and poured himself another mug of tea. In the silence that followed, I got a bit hot under the collar. I complained bitterly that I had told him the story of my life, but knew bugger all about him. He looked shocked at my cheek, and I expected a blast. Instead, he pushed his hat back and began to talk quietly as he watched Gunner over in the yard.

'It's true, Snow, I've done a lot of horse breaking. In the four years before the war I did nothing else. There's a lot of nonsense written and spoken about horse breaking, but there's no magic or great hidden secrets about it. Horse breaking is just common sense – or, at least, horse sense. Australian horse breakers have broken in tens of thousands of horses for station work and for sale overseas – and, with a few small differences, they've all used methods similar to mine. Mind you, horses are like people – you can't treat them all the same. There are colts you have to kid to and others you have to be firm with. At times you strike snags in older unbroken horses and they have to be clearly shown just who's boss.'

Chilla stopped and began to roll a smoke. Having finally got him talking about himself, I was determined to keep him going and asked him how he had got started at horse breaking.

'Well, Snow, at age thirteen I got the job of off-siding for one of the best breakers in South Australia. We broke in horses for Kidman and for the Indian army.'

Chilla pulled a boot off and inspected his toenails. Getting information from him was a bit like pulling teeth, but I was not going to give up easily. After a bit of thought, I asked him how he'd come to start work with the horse breaker.

'Well, Snow, the reason I don't talk about myself is that the past is something I'd rather forget. But, if you must know, I cleared out from home because of my father. He was a respected pillar of the local church, and one of the biggest bloody hypocrites I've known. At home he was a sadistic tyrant who made family life a hell. My sister was five years older than I was, and he disowned her when she fell in love with a Protestant lad. The lad was a decent enough bloke – anyway, they got married and cleared out to God knows where. I stuck it out for a bit longer, then left my mother and young brother to face the music on their own. I found my young brother's grave near St Quentin after the armistice. I hadn't known he was in France until the padre told me he'd been killed.'

I wondered aloud why his family hadn't told him. He looked away. 'I wrote to my mother from Egypt and again from France, but never heard back from her. My father would have burnt the letters, I reckon.'

The more Chilla told me, the more the questions seemed to arise. 'Did you go home after the war?' I asked.

'Yes, Snow, I did, but it was easier to get to the war than to return. A lot of the men who enlisted in the beginning were brought home early, but, for reasons I won't go into here, I was not among them. When I did get back, I found both my parents had died during the Spanish influenza epidemic.' My mate paused and replaced his boot.

'You see, Snow, my past is littered with ghosts. I'd rather forget the whole bloody business.'

I told him I was sorry to dredge it all up, and to change the subject, I asked him if he and his mate had returned to horse breaking.

'No, mate. Jim, the breaker I worked with, enlisted with me. He was killed two days after we landed on the Peninsula. When I came back I knew my nerve had gone, so I came over here and did a bit of shearing and other work until I met you. And that, young Snow, is the whole sorry tale.'

We smoked for a while in silence. I knew then why Chilla kept his past to himself. Anyway, we returned to the yard where Gunner was standing quietly with a slack rope. Chilla gave him another light lunging, and within half an hour the young horse was leading reasonably well. Chilla put a short halter shank on the halter. He bagged gunner again, then put the hobbles on him. I brought a pack over to the yard and Chilla showed it to the horse, then gently slipped it on his back. When he had slowly fastened the girth, breeching and breastplate, he proceeded to hang saddlecloths from the packsaddle. As a final touch, he put some stones in a kero tin and fastened that on as well.

The whole time he'd been doing this, he had kept talking to the horse. He then took off the hobbles and tied the halter shank around Gunner's neck. The young horse took the burden pretty well – after a couple of crow hops, he settled down and took little notice of the pack. Chilla put Minstrel in the yard with him for company and sat on the top rail beside me.

'A thoroughbred or Arab wouldn't take too kindly to this,' he said, nodding at Gunner, 'but this bloke has draught blood in him. That makes him a cool-blooded type. You'd have to use a collar rope to handle a lot of horses. As I said before, horses are different both in breed and in temperament.'

Chilla left the pack on the young horse for about an hour, then climbed into the yard and caught him without too much trouble. He tied him up again while we had a drink of tea, then let him go, saying he'd had enough for the first day.

Next morning we put all the horses in the big yard, then ran Gunner up into the pound. Chilla caught him without too much trouble. Gunner turned away from him once, but a flick on the rump brought him back to face up. Instead of the halter, Chilla put a bridle on Gunner this time. The young horse played with the bit as Chilla slipped his saddle on him, and then put a crupper on as well. Chilla then tied the reins back to the saddle dees and turned Gunner out with the other horses, to begin the process of mouthing him.

At smoko Chilla tightened the reins up a little, and at midday he took the bridle off and tied Gunner up once more. As we ate lunch, Chilla talked about mouthing young horses.

'Most horse breakers like to finish off mouthing by pulling a young horse around when driving the youngster in reins. I'm not totally against that, but I prefer to do the job on the horse's back. It doesn't make sense to put in a lot of time teaching a young horse to face you, then undo that by forcing the horse to turn his back on you and go away from you. It's different, of course, if you're breaking in a horse to harness.'

As soon as we'd eaten, Chilla caught Gunner and replaced the bridle with a halter. He caught Minstrel and bushed the rest of the horses. He then began to lead the young horse off Minstrel's back. If Gunner held back, a flick on the rump brought him up to the lead horse's shoulder. After he had him leading well, he took him out into the big holding yard and continued the lesson. At the end of half an hour Chilla asked me to open the yard gate and he led the young horse out into the horse paddock. Another half an hour later they returned at a trot, with Gunner keeping pace with Minstrel. Chilla then put Gunner through a short refresher course, bagging him down and picking up all four feet. He tied Gunner up during smoko, then caught him and replaced the halter with a bridle again. After letting the young horse feel his weight in the stirrup iron, Chilla slipped smoothly into the saddle. There was no great reaction from Gunner, and Chilla soon had the young horse moving around. He had to use the slack of the reins to get him going properly, but soon Gunner was being pulled around and taught to prop. Finally Chilla unsaddled him and led him over to a trough in the yards, where he washed the young horse down, then let him go. Chilla was very pleased with the progress and told me that he would ride Gunner out of the yard for the first time next day.

I've probably bored you, Simmo, with all these breaking in details, but those few days when we handled Gunner completely changed my relationship with Chilla. From that point on, we became more like mates than master and apprentice. He still continued my education, of course, but after that he gave me advice rather than a lecture.

Anyway, the next day when Chilla rode Gunner out, I went along with them on Minstrel. We went out for about an hour, with Chilla putting the young horse through his paces. We rode back to the yards at a canter, with Gunner on the bit like an old horse. When we got back, Chilla shod Gunner all round. He explained to me that during the breaking-in period a young horse becomes conditioned to accepting new experiences. It was easier to do the shoeing then than later when it had settled into a routine.

That night the common ranger paid us a visit and asked Chilla how the youngster was going.

'He's behaving like an old horse. I reckon he's ready for a bit of light work.'

'Well, you could be lucky,' said the common ranger, 'old Condamine Bill is a few days out of town with an early mob of forward stores for the trucks. He's short handed and would appreciate a hand. Why don't you take the colt out and give him a bit of work?'

We jumped at the chance, and next morning we packed Digger, and, with Chilla riding Gunner, we started out to join Condamine Bill's mob. We drove Minstrel along with the packhorse as a spare, as Chilla didn't want to overdo the youngster. We had dinner camp about twelve miles out, and after a couple of hours Chilla caught Gunner for the rest of the day. We struck Condamine's camp the next afternoon. Thirty odd horses were hobbled out and his eight packs were lined up by a good cattle camp. A fire was going behind a bough firebreak, and as we rode up a half caste chap got up from where he'd been lying under a tree.

We said good day, and he offered us a drink of tea. Chilla sipped the strong black brew and told him of our plans.

'Thank God for that, there's only been the three of us for over ten days. I'm doing the cooking and horsetailing, Bill and a kid are with the cattle.' He paused to roll a smoke. 'We've been doing three and a half hours watch each night, and the kid is dead on his feet. You'll find them on dinner camp back up the river a few miles.'

We unpacked Digger, and Chilla caught and saddled Minstrel. After hobbling the two heavier horses out, we set out to find Condamine Bill and his mob. We met them just as the bullocks were being moved off dinner camp. We both rode around and introduced ourselves to the boss drover. Condamine shook hands, pushed his hat back and gave us a hearty welcome.

'Struth, it's good to see you blokes, my word it is.'

As he and Chilla talked, I studied the drover. He was a heavily built man of about seventy, and was bald, with a ruddy face. I soon found out that without 'struth' and 'my word' he would have found it hard to hold a conversation.

We stayed with Condamine for three days and he trucked into Walgett on the fourth. I enjoyed the trip immensely. It was so different to the cow and calf droving I had done before. I was sorry to see the last of the bullocks pushed up the race into the trucks.

Late in the afternoon before we had trucked, Condamine Bill had killed a beast and given Chilla and me a whole drysalted silverside, and a side of rib bones. His mob were forward stores that had been on the road for six weeks – not the best of chewing, but Condamine had picked up a fat steer the night before. He wasn't a big beast, so didn't stand out in the mob.

After the steer was shot Condamine disposed of the brand and earmark. We had then set about cutting up the carcass on the ground, as stockmen always do. 'Struth,' said Condamine, 'look at the fat on the brisket. My word, we've got good meat here.'

Chilla was pleased with Gunner's performance, it had been valuable experience for the young horse, who had shaped up well with the cattle. Back in our camp, we hobbled the horses out, went up town for some rations, then prepared for a feast of rib bones that night. Just on sundown the jackaroo who had fallen for the con man's pitch arrived at our camp. Over a drink of tea, he asked us if we had heard of the opal miner.

'I've been trying to find him for over a week to give him that cheque,' he told us.

'Well, you're lucky you missed him,' said Chilla, 'the man was a crook. We happened to be at the railway station talking to the sergeant when he was told to leave town and never come back.

'If I were you,' Chilla went on, giving the lad a sympathetic look, 'I'd send that cheque to your mother as you first intended.'

To cheer the jackaroo up, we invited him to join us for rib bones cooked on the coals. He thanked Chilla and said he'd never eaten rib bones. Chilla looked amazed.

'What! Never eaten rib bones. Eating them is like the

first time you kiss a girl – it's an experience you'll never forget.'

What Chilla said proved to be correct, but for more than one reason. We had a huge fire going, and after the flies had departed for the night, Chilla raked out a large bed of coals. With due reverence, Chilla placed the cut-up rib bones on the coals. As they were cooked, he placed then on a mat of leaves ready beside the fire. We were about to attack them, when the lights of a car could be seen approaching. Chilla looked up from his cooking.

'That will be the bloody cops.'

The jackaroo looked nervous. 'Did you invite them?' he asked Chilla.

'No, you don't need to invite them to this kind of thing. The bastards can smell fresh beef cooking from miles away.'

The young jackaroo looked even more apprehensive. 'I don't want to get into trouble with the police. I hope these bones aren't from a stolen beast.'

Chilla gave him a stern look. 'Just relax, and leave the talking to me.'

The car pulled up and the sergeant of police, followed by a constable, got out and came over to the camp.

'Well, well,' said the sergeant, 'if it isn't Mr O'Rourke. Are these rib bones from a beast of yours?'

'Fair crack of the whip, Sergeant, you know I don't own cattle.'

'Then, I hope you can explain where these bones came from.'

'Certainly, Snowy and I gave Condamine a hand for a few days, and he gave us some meat and bones in lieu of wages.'

'Did he now? No doubt, it wasn't one of his own mob he killed.'

'I can assure you, Sergeant, that it was.'

'Can you now? Well, I'll have to check that out. I've had some dealings with the same Condamine. In the meantime, I will have to take some of those bones. They may be needed in evidence.'

'Certainly,' said Chilla, 'there's a few nice ones ready.'

The sergeant took an enormous khaki handkerchief from his pocket and selected three rib bones.

'Here's another,' offered Chilla, taking a large juicy bone off the coals.

The sergeant folded the evidence in the handkerchief, and as he was heading back to the car, told us not to leave town. The young constable stepped forward and, squatting down, reached out towards the rib bones. In a flash Chilla had his wrist in a vicelike grip. 'Piss off,' he hissed, 'you've got all the bloody evidence you're going to get here.'

'Hey, Sergeant,' bleated the constable.

The sergeant wheeled around. 'Come out of that,' he roared, 'and get in the bloody car.'

Chilla went on with the cooking as the police departed, but the young jackaroo was ashen faced when he spoke.

'It looks like we're in trouble, the police have got the evidence now.'

Chilla laughed at him. 'Evidence, my backside. That crafty old bastard will call at the first pub he comes to and bludge a bottle of beer. He'll then go back to the station and eat that evidence before it gets cold. Come on, you blokes, get these into you – stolen or not, they're bloody good.'

As I ate a rib bone, I looked at Chilla. 'Do you reckon the constable will get a bone?'

Chilla grinned. 'No, that young constable will go to bed hungry, unless he buys a pie from the pie cart.'

# 13

Snowy rolled a smoke with great deliberation, then went on with his story.

We heard no more about the rib bone affair. Chilla and I stayed in Walgett until after Anzac Day. We put in the time breaking in three young horses for the common ranger. In payment he said we could have any one of them we took a fancy to. Chilla let me pick a good-looking black mare that I had done most of the work on. To keep the name sequence going, I called her Melody. She brought our horse plant to five.

Just after Anzac Day I found a poem about the war in one of the newspapers. There was no name at the bottom of the verse and Chilla reckoned whoever wrote it had the good sense not to claim it. I've got it here somewhere.

He rummaged around in his suitcase and handed it to me. It was called 'Lost Youth'. The name of the paper was missing, and although the cutting was creased, I had no difficulty in reading it.

*LOST YOUTH*

*Medals wink in the sunshine,*
   *Ribbons weep in the rain,*
*The pipes and the drums are playing*
   *A march from an old campaign.*
*While we moulder, the lost battalions*
   *Of youth, where we long have lain.*

*We answered when England called us,*
   *From the ends of the Earth we came,*
*From the Empire's furthest outposts*

*Like moths to the candle's flame.*
*Grist for the war gods' mill wheels,*
　　*Live pawns in a monstrous game.*

*We answered the call light hearted,*
　　*Our idyll was all too brief,*
*Death stormed our days like a tempest –*
　　*Death stalked our nights like a thief,*
*And our broken, bloodied faces*
　　*Stared blindly in disbelief.*

*We lie in the sands of Sinai,*
　　*Where we fought for the age-old wells,*
*We stormed up the cliffs at Anzac*
　　*To die by the Dardanelles,*
*We fell in the mud of Flanders –*
　　*The worst of the manmade hells.*

*Like broken dolls on the wire*
　　*We died by the Somme's dark flood,*
*As the guns ploughed the 'fields of glory'*
　　*To a matrix of man and mud –*
*Where each yard of the front was purchased*
　　*By madness and human blood.*

*Attrition, the generals called it,*
　　*We learnt what attrition meant,*
*As down to the grave dark with us*
　　*Our dreams of the future went –*
*We had marched to hell in our boyhood*
　　*To die with our youth unspent.*

*We died for an English monarch,*
　　*For the sake of our 'British birth',*
*We perished that war might vanish*
　　*From the face of the tortured earth.*
*Then the 'war to end war' was over,*
　　*And the war gods rocked with mirth.*

> Medals wink in the sunshine,
>   Ribbons weep in the rain,
> The pipes and the drums are playing
>   A march from an old campaign,
> But we moulder, the lost battalions
>   Of youth, where we died in vain.

The poem bothered Chilla a bit. I suppose it reminded him of his young brother. It wasn't hard to work out that he must have enlisted at an even younger age than Chilla.

We discussed our future plans that night. Chilla said things seemed to get better the further you went from the coast. We decided to pack up and head north-west and try for work on one of the larger stations.

Before we left, a boxing show arrived in Walgett. There were quite a few of them on the road during the depression. Chilla reckoned it was one way to get a quid in hard times. 'Snowy,' he said, 'hunger is the greatest motivation there is.'

Anyway, we went along the first night, and I reckon I got carried away a bit, for when the spruiker called for volunteers to take a glove, I stuck my hand up. Chilla said I was a bloody fool, as I didn't need the quid on offer – and of course he was proved right. Another bloke, who the spruiker called a local, sang out that he'd have a go. A chorus of 'good on youse' came from the crowd when the spruiker said the two local boys would fight one another. I started to go up when they called us, but Chilla held me back.

'Hang on, I want to have a gander at this other local.'

As my opponent climbed on to the platform, Chilla hissed. 'This bloke is a plant. He's an old pro – and he's with the show. He'll know every trick in the trade, so watch yourself.'

He was a tough-looking character, but his face convinced me that he'd taken a lot of punishment, and that made me confident. I soon found out that Chilla was right. The bastard tied me up, and did everything in the clinches but bite me. I tried my best to keep away from him, but the showman let him get away with murder. In the second round he opened up my cheek with a deliberate head butt. The fight was stopped and the mauler was declared the winner.

I didn't get much sympathy from Chilla. It didn't do my self esteem much good, either, when he fought the pug the following night and knocked him out in the first round. Back up town, he gave the showman's quid to the Salvation Army.

'Snowy,' he said, 'if you ever have a spare quid, give it to the Salvos. They make better use of it than any mob I know.'

With the fisticuffs behind us, we prepared to leave Walgett. As we had no water canteens, we had purchased and broken in two sets of shoulder bags for the packhorses.

At the end of April we packed up and left Walgett on the road to Bourke. We travelled in easy stages. I rode Melody each morning, then caught Music for the rest of the day's stage. If we had a short day, Chilla saddled up Gunner and gave him a ride so that he wouldn't forget his dual role. In a week or so we were in Brewarrina. Chilla seemed intent on getting as far away from the seat of government as possible, for after a day's spell we went on towards Bourke. It did seem to me that out there the effects of the depression were not as noticeable.

Most of the stations were busy mustering. We may have been able to pick up work, but Chilla was determined to go further out. We left Bourke, and a few days later, we were in Ford's Bridge. We heard there that a big station up on Cuttaburra Creek was putting on a horse breaker and were going to start another cattle camp. Chilla looked at me. 'I think, Snowy, we've found what we've been searching for.'

Four days later we camped back from the station, then packed up and rode in next morning. As we reached the yards, I saw a crowd perched around the rails. It looked as though a bit of action was expected. Chilla and I tied up the horses and walked over. We climbed onto the top rail of the yard, where we saw that everyone's attention was directed at a bloke who was saddling a chestnut mare. Chilla asked the stockman beside him what was going on.

'Well, that mare was broken in two years ago but was never

worked. I think the boss is trying out the new horse breaker.'

Chilla never said anything, but I could see he was doing a bit of thinking. The horse breaker had the saddle on at last, but showed no inclination to follow it onto the mare's back. He finally stood back and kicked dust under the mare. She put in two spectacular bucks, then stopped. I heard Chilla whistle softly through his teeth. The mare was standing in a corner of the yard, when I heard Chilla say as if to himself. 'That mare can buck, and she's not going to knock herself about until he gets on her.'

The horse breaker caught the mare without enthusiasm, I thought, and after mucking around with her, finally got on her. He never really even looked like riding her. She caught him getting on and never let up. On the third buck, she threw him as clean as a whistle. He got up cursing and ran to the rails, where he grabbed a whip and made for the mare standing in the corner of the yard. With another curse, he brought the whip down across her rump. He was raising the whip again, when Chilla left the rails and in one bound had grasped his arm. The breaker swung around. 'What the hell ... ?'

Chilla took the whip from him. 'The only place to flog a horse is from its back. If you're not capable of that, don't do it at all.'

The horse breaker tried to release his arm. 'Get out of this yard. I'm the breaker here – ask the boss.'

'To hell with you and your boss,' Chilla said, and whirling the breaker around, he ran him over to the rails and almost threw him through them. He turned then and walked slowly over to the mare. He spoke so softly to her that I could barely hear him. With slow deliberate actions, he caught her, reined her up and, in one fluid movement that was almost too fast to see, was in the saddle.

I've seen some great rides in my time, Simmo – that mare could coil, but old Chilla never looked like being thrown. As I watched an exhibition of real horsemanship, I thought to myself that if Chilla had ever lost his nerve, he had regained it that day. He rode the mare to a standstill, then, after patting her neck, he cantered her around the yard. Finally he reined her up, and looking at the crowd on the rails he spoke. 'Who's the manager here?'

A smartly dressed bloke on the rails replied, 'I am, and just who the hell are you?'

'My name's O'Rourke, and I've broken in more horses than that breaker of yours has had hot dinners. My mate and I will break in your horses, if you wish. If not, keep the useless, horse-murdering bastard you've got.'

Chilla got off the mare and looked up at the boss. 'Is there a tap around here where I can wash this mare down?'

The manager, who was still a bit dumbfounded by Chilla's outburst, jerked his thumb towards a trough in a holding yard. I walked over to Chilla as he unsaddled the mare and led her over to the trough. As we were washing her down, a jackaroo came over. He said the manager had told him to take us to the men's kitchen for smoko.

'Well,' said Chilla, 'we'll get a drink of tea out of the place, anyway.'

The ringer's kitchen was a large galvanised-iron building. A huge slow-combustion stove, together with benches and cupboards, occupied one end, the rest was taken up by a long table with bench seats on each side. Smoko was apparently over, but the cook came over and slammed a plate of brownies and a large teapot in front of us.

'The bloody boss must think I'm running a flamin' do-drop-inn here,' he snarled.

Chilla grinned at him. 'Well, if you were, you'd have plenty of customers with brownies like this.'

The way to any bush cook's heart is to praise his brownie. At once the babbler's attitude changed. He looked at Chilla. 'Are you the bloke who rode that mare in the yard?'

Chilla nodded, and the cook continued. 'Well, I hope the boss sacks that jackaroo he's employed as a breaker. The bastard couldn't ride his swag on a windy day, if you ask me. You know the bloody upstart asked me if I could make a cake – a bloody cake, when there's brownies like that.'

Still fuming, the cook retreated to the other end of the

building. He was a tough-looking old character – he had a mermaid tattooed on one forearm and a sea serpent on the other. We learnt later that he claimed to have sailed before the mast. I suppose he could have, too. Lads went to sea at a tender age in the days of sail. As we walked out of the kitchen, Chilla said, 'Well, at least we've got the cook on side.'

The jackaroo told us to go up to the office, where we found the manager and bookkeeper in conference. They looked up as we entered. The boss didn't beat about the bush.

'There's forty-odd horses here to be broken. Some have to go to another station. I can give you five bob a head and station wages for one man.'

'Well,' said Chilla, 'I dare say the bloke you had would have agreed to those terms. We'll take the job on for ten bob a head, plus station wages and keep for both of us. I can guarantee your colts will be well broken and shod all round.'

The manager hummed and hahed for a minute, but having sacked his first choice, he was up the creek without a paddle. He finally agreed, telling us there was plenty of breaking-in tackle in the saddle room.

'Right,' said Chilla. 'Just one other thing – I won't stand for any interference. Judge the finished product, if you wish, but leave us alone to do the job.'

Before the manager had a chance to answer, Chilla was out the door. We checked over the breaking-in gear, and that afternoon, with the help of a couple of stockmen, we mustered the young horses out of the home horse paddock. Chilla sat on the rails of the receiving yard and looked them over. They were all three- and four-year-olds – bloody good sorts, too. Chilla was delighted with them. There was no sign of the nerves he had previously mentioned, and he appeared to be happy to be back doing the work he knew so well.

We drafted out four of the youngsters to catch next day, and after letting them go in the large night paddock, we took the rest back to where we had mustered them from.

175

Right from the start, Chilla used Gunner as a breaking-in horse, and he took to the job like a duck to water. There were very few snags amongst the breakers and we were soon handling over six every week. As a result, we often had ten or so colts in hand, and Chilla encouraged me to do more and more of the riding. When taking breakers out on the second ride, Chilla liked to educate them by riding up around the station buildings.

The manager had a couple of kids aged about five and six, and a governess was employed to teach them correspondence lessons. Often she had the two tykes out on the back verandah when I rode young horses past. I couldn't resist doing a bit of lairising, and sometimes I thumbed up a lively colt before I rode around the corner of the house. Chilla would have gone crook if he'd known. He wouldn't let a colt drop its head if it could be avoided.

One day I rode a big grey colt out – Chilla reckoned he had a dash of arab in him. As I went past the back verandah, the kids waved their hats at us. Well, that bastard gave me the ride of my life. I hung on to him, but only just. To have been thrown would have been the biggest shame, but the kids and the governess cheered and clapped until the bastard bucked behind an outbuilding.

The next time I rode him out, I gave him heaps before going near the station.

During the second week we were there, the manager came and saw me. He said he had a pony he had bought for the kids to use later on, but they were still too young to get on a horse, in his opinion. The governess, however, had indicated that she would like to do a spot of riding. He explained that she had ridden a little, but added that the pony would need a few rides to make sure he was suitable. He finally got around to asking me to give the pony a bit of work.

The next time we ran breakers in from the horse paddock, I drafted the pony out and put him with the breakers in the night paddock. He was more galloway than pony, and as quiet as a bloody mouse – you could crawl all over him. A week later the boss came and saw me and asked me if I would take the governess out for a ride – if I thought the pony was ready. I wondered why he didn't ask one of the jackaroos to do the honours, but being young and flattered, I agreed. I told Chilla about it that night, but he didn't seem overjoyed.

'Be careful not to let sex raise its ugly head, Snowy, my lad. There's no room for romance in the round yard.'

Anyway, on Sunday, Colleen – that was her name – and I went for a ride down along the creek flats. The pony behaved himself and she managed him quite well. She rode astride, but that was before women took to wearing slacks. What she had on was, I think, called a riding habit. Anyway, you could have made a bloody tent out of the material in it. She was a friendly type of girl, and one who, like all females, asked a lot of questions. I told her very little about myself, playing the quiet stockman for all I was worth. One of the few things I've learnt about women, Simmo, is that being mysterious drives 'em wild. The less you tell 'em, the more intrigued they are.

Pretty soon I was taking her out on the pony some evenings after we finished for the day. I didn't mind, as it kept Melody in work. Despite Colleen not knowing a lot about me, we became quite friendly. She was a pretty little thing, but I remembered Chilla's advice and didn't make any advances.

Chilla and I had decided to head up into Queensland after we finished the breaking in. Things were better there, we had heard. Chilla was sure we would get work on the Channel Country stations. We planned to hand over the last of the colts on a Monday and start north the following day.

We finished work on the youngsters on the Saturday. Early on the Sunday morning Colleen met me leaving the kitchen after breakfast. She told me the manager had given her permission to go out on a picnic with me that day. It hit me for six, I can tell you. I could see the look of anticipation leave her face at my hesitation. Then I thought, what the hell, I'll be on the road to Queensland in two days time. I watched her face light up as I agreed to meet her with the horses at ten o'clock.

I told Chilla of the arrangement, expecting him to be against the whole thing. He gave me one of his fatherly looks. 'You've got me to thank for that. The boss asked me if you could be trusted, so don't let me down.'

I find it hard to describe how I felt at that time. I was sort of elated and at the same time apprehensive. Anyway, I ran Music and the pony in and saddled them both, and at ten I led the pony up to the front gate of the big house. Colleen came out dressed in her riding habit and wearing a straw hat. In one hand she was carrying a billy can and in the other a large wicker hamper. I grinned at her and asked her how long we were going away for.

She blushed and stammered, 'Well, I-I . . .'

I told her I was only joking and that we'd manage all right. I dismounted and after helping her on the pony, I hung the billy on the fence, telling her I had a quart pot on my saddle that would do. The basket was a bit of a problem, but I balanced it on a post and decided to pick it up after mounting Music. The mare shied away from it a couple of times, but I managed to get it onto the pommel and we set off.

The stockmen had told me about a small creek that flowed out of some rough hills. The spot was about six miles from the station. I told Colleen of the place and she said it sounded ideal. She chatted happily as we rode along, and I felt I'd been stupid for having initial doubts about the excursion. We found the creek and rode up it until we reached a spot where it left the hills. It was a bloody beautiful place. The little creek fell over a low, rocky ledge into a deep boulder-strewn pool. It was a secluded spot with thick scrub all around, and seemed like a friendly little world all of its own.

We explored the creek for some time, then prepared for the picnic. While I lit a fire, Colleen opened up the monstrous hamper and spread a rug under the shade of a tree. On it she placed enough sandwiches and cakes for four people.

The boiling of the quart intrigued her, and I had to explain all its virtues to her. I made the tea, then we both settled down to do justice to the picnic fare. Fortunately the ants stayed away, but a pair of magpies with two half-grown young arrived. Colleen was fascinated by the antics of the young birds as they squawked for their parents to feed them. She threw them bits of bread and meat and was delighted to see her offerings accepted with gusto.

After we had eaten, I rolled a smoke and lay back at peace with the world. I lazily watched Colleen pack up the hamper. I think she would have liked to fold up the rug, but I wasn't going to be moved just then. She watched the magpies take off, then went down to the hole and skipped some flat stones across the water. I was lying back at ease, when she called out. 'Come on, Snowy, there's some small fish and shrimps in the shallows here. Let's see if we can catch some.'

Colleen was obviously bent on getting full value out of the picnic. I went down and, sure enough, I saw the tiddlers and little shrimp-like things she had mentioned. They were darting about in the shallow water just below the cascade. I pulled off my boots and rolled my duds up and paddled about in an attempt to grab one. The bottom was sandy, but there were boulders under which the little blighters escaped. Before long, Colleen had taken off her stockings and shoes and joined me. She splashed about with obvious delight and I suddenly realised how much the outing meant to her. It must have been a God-sent opportunity to escape from the humdrum life at the station.

Despite her best efforts, she couldn't catch one. Of course, the riding habit restricted her movements – the damn thing almost reached her ankles. She held it up with one hand and was able to keep it reasonably dry, until she slipped on a mossy boulder and half fell in. She stood up and, without any false modesty, said, 'Shut your eyes, Snowy, I'm taking this thing off.'

I did what she asked, although it seemed strange to me that seeing her take it off was worse than seeing her without it. She still had plenty on, of course. Women's underclothes were fairly substantial those days.

Anyway, we mucked around there and splashed water on ourselves like a pair of kids. Then she fell into a deep hole, and as I put a hand out to help her, she pulled me in, too. She thought that was a great joke and said that as we were both wet, we might as well have a swim. I took off my shirt and threw it out on the bank to dry, then swam after her. We played and swam and tagged each other – all innocent fun. But then the inevitable happened.

It all seemed so natural, neither of us said anything. I think if one of us had spoken, the spell would have been broken. There was just the two of us and that little creek. It was as if the rest of the world had vanished.

Later we lay on the bank and watched a kingfisher dive into our waterhole. Colleen had her head in the crook of my arm. She kissed me on the cheek and started to sing softly as if to herself. I think that moment was as close to Heaven as I'll ever get. In a sweet voice, she sang old songs I'd never heard before. And then ... and then I went to bloody sleep.

When I woke up, it was the governess who stood beside me, riding habit and all. Without looking at me, she said, 'Snowy, I think it's time we went back. Would you mind saddling the horses?'

I got up, found my duds and did what she asked. She never spoke on the way back to the station, and I was afraid to, in case I said the wrong thing. At the garden gate at the homestead, I slipped off Music and held the pony as she dismounted. She took the hamper from me and went to the gate. She turned, then, and, with a funny look on her face, said, 'Snowy, I will never forget you.'

I'll never know, Simmo, if she did or not – but one thing I can tell you, I'll never forget her.

My mate stopped talking – the silence lasted so long I looked over and found that he was asleep. I silently stubbed out my cigarette and followed his example.

*It was as if the rest of the world had vanished.*

The noise of the fencers' truck starting up woke me just on daylight. I sat up and looked over at Snowy's bunk. The mattress was bare, and the wardrobe stood open and empty. I jumped up and turned on the light. There was a page out of his notebook on the bed. I read it as the truck engine faded.

'Sorry, Simmo, got to go. Square things off with Maisie for me, if you can. Good luck. Snowy.'

Chilla's apprentice had gone with the coming of the dawn.

# Glossary

## General

| | |
|---|---|
| bit between the teeth | refused to stop |
| crack a lay | give the show away |
| crow hop | ineffectual bucks |
| dingo (verb) | cease to resist |
| do a bolt | clear out |
| doss | sleep or rest |
| fair dinkum | true or correct |
| flea in someone's ear | a warning |
| frog and toad | road |
| gander | a look |
| give someone the drum | tell someone what is happening |
| go to ground | hide |
| grouse | very good |
| have a dinner camp | sleep |
| have a snout on someone | hold a grudge |
| kip | a sleep; or a small piece of wood used to toss pennies in two-up |
| knock up | become exhausted |
| lit out | cleared out, escaped |
| lurk (noun) | a ruse or plan to deceive |
| moolah | money |
| packing them | being afraid |
| pick up the drift | understand what is being said |
| pig weed | a native succulent weed |
| plant (noun) | an object or person placed to deceive |
| plant (verb) | to hide |
| posh | the best |
| provos | military police |
| pull on | have a go |
| put the fangs in | ask for money |

| | |
|---|---|
| shoot through | clear out |
| snavel | steal |
| stony | broke, without money |
| stunt | name given by first world war diggers to any AIF attack |
| struth | short for God's truth |
| swy | two-up |
| take a shine to | like |
| under the weather | drunk or sick |
| wallopers | police |

## Currency

| | |
|---|---|
| bob | shilling (equivalent to 10 cents in those days) |
| brick | 10 pounds (equivalent to 20 dollars in those days) |
| pence | roughly equivalent to 1 cent in those days |
| pound/quid | equivalent to 2 dollars in those days |
| sixpence/zack | equivalent to 5 cents in those days |

## Other measurements

| | |
|---|---|
| acre | 0.4 hectares |
| dozen | 12 of an item |
| foot | 30 centimetres |
| inch | 2.5 centimetres |
| mile | 1.6 kilometres |
| pound (weight) | 0.45 kilograms |
| yard | just under a metre; about 90 centimetres |

# Notes

'Big Fella' — Jack Lang

Douglas Credit — a revolutionary monetary system introduced by the government of Alberta, an independent province of Canada, in the early thirties. It was also known as Social Credit. Pressure from world banks and the second world war saw its demise

'Kevin Barry' song — a banned Irish rebels' song

# Sources of Background Material

Adam-Smith, Patsy. *The Anzacs*, Thomas Nelson Australia, West Melbourne, 1978.

Bean, C.E.W. *The Official History of Australia in the War of 1914–1918: The A.I.F. in France 1918 Volume VI*, Angus and Robertson, Sydney, 1941.

Cannon, Michael. *The Human Face of the Great Depression*, published by the author, PO Box 598, Mornington, Vic 3931, 1996.

Davison, Graeme, John Hirst and Stuart Macintyre. *The Oxford Companion to Australian History*, Oxford University Press, Melbourne, 1998.

Gammage, Bill. *The Broken Years*, Penguin, Ringwood 1974.

Hearn, Mark and Harry Knowles. *One Big Union*, Cambridge University Press, 1996.

Laffin, John. *Australians At War: Western Front 1917–1918, The Cost of Victory*, Time Life Books in association with John Ferguson, Sydney, 1988.

Lang, J.T. *The Great Bust*, McNamara's Books, Leura, 1980.

Legrand, Jacques. *Chronicle of the 20th Century*. Chronicle Australia, Ringwood, 1990.

Lloyd, Clem and Jacqui Rees. *The Last Shilling*, Melbourne University Press, Carlton, 1994.

Lowenstein, Wendy. *Weevils in the Flour*, Hyland House, Melbourne, 1978.

Masson, Mick. *Surviving the Dole Years*, New South Wales University Press, 1993.

Troughton, Ellis. *Furred Animals of Australia*, Angus and Robertson, Sydney, 1941.